CRICKET
THE MEN
AND THE
MATCHES
THAT CHANGED
THE GAME

CRICKET
THE MEN
AND THE
MATCHES
THAT CHANGED
THE GAME

ALLEN SYNGE

Foreword by Brian Johnston

St Michael

ACKNOWLEDGEMENTS

Time and again, as I reached for the shelf to check a date or a score, I found a cricket book inscribed to me by my father, the late Robert Millington Synge, on the occasion of passing some exam or other. I am much in his debt for this wealth of reference and, indeed, for a lasting enthusiasm which my father directly inspired.

I am similarly indebted to my uncle, Richard Cave, for a rich cricket archive and a grandstand seat at many Test matches long ago.

I am extremely grateful to Derek Anns, my partner in another cricket history, for much invaluable material and advice; also to Audrey Nicholson, Yorkshire's unofficial archivist, for vital clues to players and games that have influenced the course of cricket.

A.S.

This edition published for
Marks and Spencer plc in 1988
by Century Benham Ltd, Brookmount House,
62–65 Chandos Place, London WC2N 4NW

Copyright © Allen Synge 1988

ISBN 0 7126 2483 X

Designed by Bob Burroughs
Typeset in Plantin medium roman
by Vision Typesetting, Manchester
Printed and bound in Great Britain by
Butler and Tanner, Frome and London

COVER PHOTOGRAPHS

FRONT: *top row* – Imran Khan (Pakistan), W.G. Grace (Eng.), Mike Brearley (Eng.); *bottom row* – Malcolm Marshall (WI), Dennis Lillee (Aus.), Sunil Gavaskar (India).

BACK: Ian Botham *v* Australia, Richard Hadlee (NZ), Tony Greig (Eng.), Gary Sobers (WI).

CONTENTS

FOREWORD

I have enjoyed this book immensely. It's a fascinating study of the evolution of cricket throughout the last two hundred and fifty years or so. Allen Synge has divided his analysis into different categories and comes up with well thought out, sensible, and in some cases, original conclusions.

The development of bowling starts with the devastating lobs of David Harris of Hambledon, followed by the roundarm revolution of the Kent amateur John Willes in 1822. Roundarm bowling became legal twenty years later, as did overarm bowling after Edgar Willsher had had a slight 'local difficulty' with umpire John Lillywhite. There followed the introduction of swing by a gentleman of Philadelphia, 'Bart' King, and then the biggest sensation of all – B.J.T. Bosanquet's googly.

As bowling developed the batsmen had to devise strokes to combat it, and Allen Synge picks out some of the originators: Ranji with the leg-flick, Fuller Pilch with the off-drive, and Felix with the cut. For a time hitting a ball to leg was *non-U*. But George Parr showed how productive in runs the leg-side could be, and the great W.G. Grace himself favoured the pull stroke to leg from balls outside the off-stump. Leg-side hitting received a further boost after Walter Read's sensational 117 when batting No. 10 for England at the Oval in 1884.

The unwitting law-creators make an interesting bunch. John Ring of Kent was 'shabby enough' to put his legs deliberately in front of the bowler's deliveries, and the LBW law followed. The crafty White of Ryegate used a bat the same width as the stumps. As a result the present width of the bat ($4\frac{1}{4}''$) was made law. So was the addition of a middle stump after Lumpy Stevens, the Kent underarm bowler, had bowled several balls through the then two stumps when John Small was batting at the Artillery Ground. There came later alterations due to the activities of various individuals. Douglas Jardine's Bodyline Tour was primarily responsible for the law against intimidation of batsmen.

Sid Barnes' incessant appeals against the light on a brilliant sunny day in Australia brought in the appeal against the light legislation. The blatant chucky of Meckiff and Rorke in 1958/59 and Rorke's flagrant drag were the major reasons in the laws on throwing and the introduction of the front foot law.

Allen Synge also makes an interesting list of the people who have most influenced the game, ranging from Lord Harris, Lord Hawke and Sir Pelham Warner to batsmen like W.G. Grace, Don Bradman, Jack Hobbs, Wally Hammond, Denis Compton, Ian Botham and Viv Richards. I can already hear shouts of protest from Yorkshire of 'what about, Sutcliffe, Hutton and Boycott?!' Allen also makes an interesting accusation against Warwick Armstrong, Douglas Jardine, Don Bradman, Len Hutton and Clive Lloyd, for bringing 'war' into cricket. I expect you can see why. They were all responsible for favouring double-speed attacks with the object – not openly admitted – of bringing intimidation into cricket.

There are so many other interesting things to read, digest, enjoy and in some cases to disagree with. These range from the changing fashions in dress, the status of umpires and the effects of the arrival of the one-day game.

I hope that Gatting, Botham and co. will get a copy of this book so that they can learn about the origin of the reverse sweep. Allen Synge claims that the originator was Sir Timothy O'Brien of Middlesex, a fiery giant of an Irishman who was a big hitter of the ball. He was batting one day at Lord's against Gloucestershire and E.M. and W.G. Grace were fielding at point and slip. They were chatting to each other in a loud voice trying to put Sir Timothy off his stroke. He got so annoyed that when a ball pitched on his leg stump he quickly did a reverse sweep when they were least expecting a hit in their direction. The ball is said to have hit W.G. hard in his mid-riff but whether it stopped him talking is not related. I rather doubt if it did!

Brian Johnston

THE MEN

1
FIVE GREAT DICTATORS OF CHANGE

A game of cricket is a variety show which, on a good day, will put many different talents on view: magicians of spin and masters of pace, acrobatic close-fielders and, in the outfield, athletes with prodigious throwing arms. But for most of us, it's batting that tops the bill. The records suggest that over the years vastly more people have deserted their offices to see the Graces, Bradmans and Bothams bat than have risked dismissal to watch bowlers of equal stature in action.

The reason, of course, is that batting is an unrivalled variety show in itself. Compared with baseball, say, it offers at least eleven recognized scoring strokes to the US striker's single, repetitive, cross-batted swipe. And that's without attempting to catalogue all the individual variations the greats can add to the repertoire, or trying to list the shots that a one-day batsman will improvise in order to keep up with the clock.

To whom does the great batsman owe his impressive armoury of strokes? Ironically enough, it is to a character with whom he is not always on the best of terms – the inventive bowler. If we leaf through the pages of cricket history we are bound to notice how often it was a new challenge from the popping crease that forced batsmen into developing the footwork and range of strokes that have given the art its wonderful variety. It could be argued that without bowlers who were prepared to explore new methods of curtailing an innings, batsmen might still be wearing top hats! Let us look a little closer at just five of cricket's 'great dictators of change'.

THE WICKED TRAJECTORY OF DAVID HARRIS

Our first formidable innovator could literally be heard knocking on the door of cricket history – a barn door, as it happened. This was David Harris, the genial but devastating underarm bowler of the Hambledon Cricket Club. One dark winter's night in the early 1780s, strange sounds were reported to be emanating from a barn in the village of Crookham in Hampshire. A new-fangled threshing device? Or something very nasty in the woodshed? Investigation showed that the rafters were actually ringing from the methodical deliveries of a bowler who was to become a legend for practising and perfecting his art, day and night, in season and out, come sun, rain or snow. As a bachelor, Harris had plenty of winter evenings to spare, and in his case practice seems to have made almost perfect. During one season at Broad-Halfpenny Down (Hambledon's famous home ground) he is reputed to have worn a bald spot on the wicket with the precision of his length.

Yet Harris posed more severe problems than simply those of nagging accuracy. Unlike any underarm bowler hitherto, he added the menace of wickedly sharp lift. Nobody ever quite succeeded in fathoming the

Hambledon's David Harris. A detail from George Shepherd's sketch made at Lord's around 1790.

Hambledon re-visited. Modern cricketers play at Harris and Fennex on Broad Halfpenny Down.

secret of Harris' craft, but its broad outlines could be discerned by any nervously waiting batsman. Harris would begin his run 'erect as a soldier', with the ball held at full stretch above his head. Springing to the wicket with a disconcerting whirling action he would produce the ball, as if from nowhere, at chest height, imparting a savage, last-second twist that could send it leaping at the batsman's ungloved fingers before he realized what was about to hit him. Most of the scores of the early Hambledon period are missing, but we know that in an innings total of around 70–80 (about par for the course at that time), a maximum of 8 or 9 would have been scored off the affable potter of Crookham.

What was the answer to this deadly combination of immaculate length, deceptive flight and bruising lift from the wicket? For a time, even the most belligerent batsmen were forced on to the defensive – not the easiest of postures in those days since the Hambledon-style bat, like its baseball descendant, was fashioned for the offensive. Harris reaped a bumper harvest of catches behind the wicket.

It took a Buckinghamshire-born all-rounder named William Fennex to perceive that there was another option, which was to get out to the pitch of the ball and drive. Up until now batsmen had tended to stand with two feet firmly rooted athwart the blockhole. In leaving the crease to knock David Harris off his length, Fennex blazed a trail down which Beldam and Fuller Pilch would follow and Ranji, Jessop, Hammond and our own Botham would eventually come dancing.

William Fennex lived to the age of seventy-five, by no means a record by Hambledonian standards yet long enough to secure his claim to the title of 'father of forward play'. But if necessity is the mother of invention, then the true originator of this style must be regarded as having been that dedicated bachelor, David Harris.

THE ROUND-ARM REVOLUTIONARY

The story of our second 'change dictator' can be briefly told, if only because his playing career was brought to a sadly premature conclusion.

The tombstone of John Willes in Sutton Valence churchyard.

The Kent amateur John Willes was the spearhead of a revolutionary movement which aimed to raise the bowling arm from trouser-pocket level to shoulder height and possibly higher. Certainly the movement was calculated to raise eyebrows. 'I am decidedly of the opinion,' huffed John Nyren, 'that if the custom be not stopped the character of the game will be changed.'

A contemporary match report in the *Morning Herald* suggests one good reason for the Establishment's qualms. 'The straight-armed bowling introduced by John Willes Esq. was generally practised in this game and proved a great obstacle against getting runs.'

Willes was definitely fast enough to make enemies in influential batting circles, and like all pioneers of change he was to suffer both frustration and persecution. We read that he was banned from a number of cricket grounds and that elsewhere unruly pitch invasions disrupted matches in which he was taking part.

The climax came when Kent met the MCC at Lord's on 15 July 1822. Willes opened the bowling for his county and was immediately no-balled by umpire Noah Mann, the son of a former Hambledon player. Sensing that officialdom's finger was finally raised against him, Willes is reported to have tossed down the ball in disgust and left the game for good in favour of other sports and pastimes.

Who was behind the professional assassination of John Willes? The evidence points towards an early patron of cricket, and no mean batsman, William Ward. We know that he was hostile to the new bowling and that he was on record as being 'unable to play it'. Moreover, he was in the process of negotiating the lease of Lord's cricket ground and was therefore in a position to influence the judgement of the honest Noah, the rules being technically hazy on the subject of the round-arm delivery.

In the long run, Willes was not to die a disappointed man. He lived to see players such as William Lillywhite carry the round-arm revolution to the threshold of today's fast overarm bowling and all the thrills that batting against the lifting ball can offer the spectator. Meanwhile, even William Ward relented, admitting that the new bowling was necessary since 'all the old bowlers were used up'.

The round-arm revolution became so respectable that other candidates were advanced as having been its initiators. 'Tom Walker tried what Nyren calls the throwing ball,' wrote the early cricket historian the Reverend John Mitford, 'and defied all the players of the day to withstand this novelty . . . but Willes, a Kent man, had all the praise of inventing it some twenty years later.' Willes, however, took care to establish his claim in indelible form. The epitaph on his tombstone in Sutton Valence churchyard reads: 'He was a patron of all manly sports and the first to introduce round-arm bowling in cricket.'

B.J.T. BOSANQUET – THE PUZZLE MASTER

The scene is Lord's on another July day. The year is 1900 and Middlesex are playing Leicestershire. A young man, recently down from Oxford, comes on to bowl for Middlesex. His first few deliveries are orthodox leg-breaks which are played without difficulty. Then the moment arrives for the test flight. The ball slips from the bowler's

Spot the googly! An artist's impression of B.J.T. Bosanquet in action.

fingers and ground-hops along the pitch like a Wright brothers' flying machine, bouncing four times. Sam Coe, Leicestershire's dependable left-hander, goes down the wicket to give this apology of a leg-break the punishment it deserves and hears the wicket-keeper howl an appeal as the bails fly. Sam Coe is out stumped, and on his way into the records as the first authenticated victim of the 'googly', although back in the pavilion he will doubtless call it by another name.

The fielders do not crowd around to embrace a bowler in these more formal times. There may even be heard faint murmurs of disapproval from the gentlemen among the players. But the author of Coe's destruction, Mr B.J.T. Bosanquet, is almost certainly wearing a broad smile, for the father of ITN's late, lamented Reggie Bosanquet is nothing if not a humorous man. Besides, he has finally proved that his tactic works!

The story of the invention of the 'googly', 'wrong-'un' or 'bosie', as the Australians call it to this day, has many versions. According to one it was developed on the green baize of the billiard table. Another has Bosanquet's girl cousin acting as guinea pig as waywardly bouncing tennis balls are spun down to her through many a long summer afternoon. In yet another version, the ball that looks like a leg-break but turns out to be the reverse was a by-product of the game of 'Twisti-Twosti', another Bosanquet novelty – this one designed for passing the time on wet afternoons in the pavilion. But the truth of the matter was, surely, that Bosanquet's itchy fingers could never resist an opportunity to make a spherical shape behave perversely. 'Some other experimental beggars may have fooled about with the googly,' he confided to R.C. Robertson-Glasgow in later years, 'but it was I that put the thing on the market; and it sold – oh yes, it sold a good many!'

Back in the season of 1900, Bosanquet and his googly went on to take a number of famous scalps, including that of Nottinghamshire's William Gunn. 'This bowling is unfair', protested his county colleague Arthur Shrewsbury. 'Not unfair – just immoral', Bosanquet wisecracked in return.

England in Australia, 1903/4. P.F. Warner is seated front row, centre. Bosanquet is on his right.

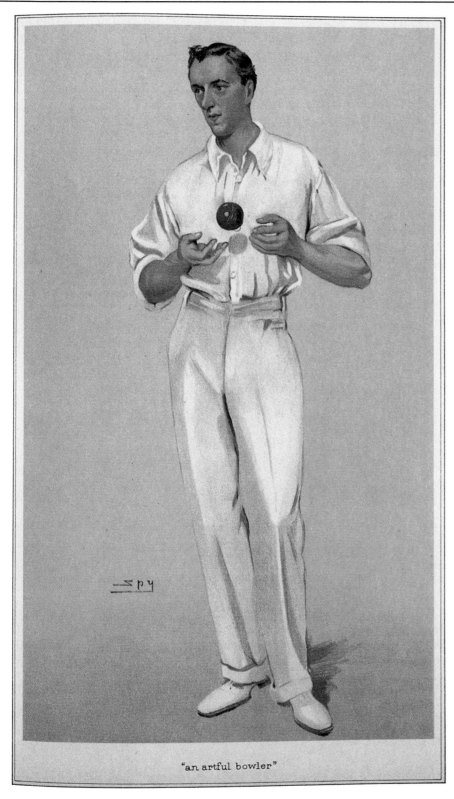

"an artful bowler"

B.J.T. Bosanquet – a controversial member of P.F. Warner's 1903/4 touring party.

There remained the problem of length, over which B.J.T. could never guarantee to exercise total control. This was possibly why, when his name was announced among the party to tour Australia in 1903/4, he attracted the fullest fury of what the captain, P.F. Warner, described as 'a hail of press criticism and disapprobation'. Warner himself was accused of blatant favouritism towards a Middlesex colleague, and for the time being could only point to Bosanquet's usefulness with the bat (he twice scored a century in each innings for Middlesex at Lord's).

Despite the media's misgivings, Warner's 1903 tourists set out from St Pancras station with a send-off unparalleled even in our multi-tour, jet-aeroplane era. 'There could not have been more noise if Jessop had hit twelve fours in two overs', one witness reported. The background was an England at the height of its swaggering imperial power, still smarting from defeat in the 1902 Test series, which by any objective comparison of resources should have been won, and in particular from Fred Tate's fateful dropped catch in Australia's three-run victory in the Fourth Test at Manchester.

Bosanquet had already signalled a warning to Australian batting. Passing through Sydney on the way home from New Zealand with Lord Hawke's touring party early in 1903, he had knocked back Victor Trumper's middle stump with a ball that still had no recognized name.

Now, six months later at Sydney with Australia chasing 329 to level the series, Bosanquet and his invention entered into Test history. 'As was my unfailing custom,' reports the prolific yet taciturn writer, Warner, 'I brought Bosanquet on a quarter of an hour before the tea interval.' The aim, presumably, was to limit Australia's chances of collaring him. Warner need not have worried. This is how the scorecard read for Australia's second innings in the Fourth Sydney Test.

V.T. Trumper	lbw b Arnold	12
R.A. Duff	b Arnold	19
C. Hill	st Lilley b Bosanquet	26
P.A. McAlister	b Hirst	1
A.J. Hopkins	st Lilley b Bosanquet	0
C.E. McLeod	c Lilley b Bosanquet	6
J.J. Kelly	c Foster b Bosanquet	10
M.A. Noble	not out	53
S.E. Gregory	lbw b Bosanquet	0
H. Trumble	st Lilley b Bosanquet	0
A. Cotter	b Hirst	34
Byes		10
	Total	171

Bosanquet's figures were 15 overs, 1 maiden, 51 runs, 6 wickets.

The Ashes were regained, and on the 'golden evening' of his cricket career Warner recalled the bitter criticisms that had been levelled against him and Bosanquet, and felt able to assert, 'On hard wickets he is the most difficult bowler in the world.'

Bosanquet was to have one more afternoon of Test glory when he took eight Australian second-innings wickets in the First Test at Nottingham in 1905. Yet by the Fourth Test he had lost his place and was not to reappear in international cricket. Batsmen, however, continued to be plagued by his googly every season up to the First World War and beyond. By 1911, for example, Australia had produced their own 'bosie' specialist in the person of H.V. Horden, 'a bowler of well nigh perfect length lacking Bosanquet's erraticism'. (Warner again.) Horden was to win a Test match almost single-handedly with figures of 5 for 85 and 7 for 90 in England's two innings in the first encounter between the two countries that Australian season.

Meanwhile, an occasional Middlesex player of military medium pace had been studying Bosanquet's technique at first hand and secretly perfecting his own variation on the theme of the last-second finger flick. His name was R.O. Schwarz, a South African who on return to his own country would find a responsive surface for Bosanquet's borrowed invention on the matting wickets which were standard there. When P.F. Warner arrived with his 1905/6 MCC tourists, he was met with liberal doses of the medicine he had dished out to Australia two winters before. Schwarz now headed a quartet of 'bosie' bowlers – himself, Faulkner, Vogler and White – who were to make a nightmare of batting on matting. England were not at full strength, yet they were strong enough in the view of the selectors to keep a novice Test nation in its place. In

R.O. Schwarz of Middlesex and South Africa – an inspired imitator of his county colleague's revolutionary style.

the event, however, the tourists went down to a humiliating four to one defeat.

Eventually the top batsmen of the period, notably Hobbs and Rhodes, were to learn to detect the slight alteration of foot or arm movement that betrayed the googly in the act of delivery. But the ball had introduced an intriguing guessing game to cricket, although not necessarily to its benefit in some views. Neville Cardus suggests that the googly destroyed the glorious uncertainties of golden-age cricket, producing batsmen who either stayed watchfully in their crease or leapt, sometimes foolhardily, down the wicket. Once again, innovative bowling had prodded batsmen into seeking new methods of counter-attack.

AMERICA'S KING OF SWING

Bosanquet's career overlapped that of another significant innovator, but, unlike Bosanquet, he learned his cricket far from Eton, Oxford and the Nursery at Lord's. His name was John Barton King, and his cricket academy was, improbably enough, Philadelphia, USA!

It is sometimes forgotten that the city that promulgated the Declaration of Independence was once capable of throwing down a formidable cricket challenge. The Gentlemen of Philadephia, selected from a number of flourishing local clubs, toured Canada, the West Indies and England where they often overcame top county sides. They also welcomed and conquered England and Australian sides of near Test strength. From 1897 until the outbreak of the First World War their attack was spearheaded by 'Bart' King, rated by Sir Pelham Warner as one of the greatest fast bowlers of all time.

We get the impression that the Gentlemen of Philadelphia were a well-heeled lot who took their claim to gentility very seriously. King was an exception to this rule. Without inherited wealth, he had to be discreetly subsidized by richer team-mates. More to the point, he had been an above-average pitcher at baseball, a game that the cricket historian Rowland Bowen suggests the Philadelphia clubs had been created to discourage. Whatever may be said about the lack of variety in baseball batting techniques, there is no doubt that baseball pitchers were, at that time, decades ahead of their cricket counterparts in their ability to make a ball swerve or dip in flight.

Getting into his swing – John Barton King of the Gentlemen of Philadelphia.

It was by this route that 'Bart' King was to bring to his cricket not only the perils of pace but the novel threat of swing. King could move 'the angler', as he called it, into or away from the bat, usually uncomfortably late. A few statistics will convey the impact his bowling made on English cricket. In 1897 he took 7 wickets for 33 runs in an innings v Sussex at Hove (K.S. Ranjitsinhji 0, Sussex all out for 46). In 1903, at Old Trafford, he chalked up 5 wickets for 46 in Lancashire's first innings, and 9 wickets for 62 in the second. In the same season, King helped to send Surrey down by a 110-run defeat at The Oval with 6 wickets and scores of 98 and 113 in the Philadelphians' two innings. In 1908, at the age of thirty-five, he headed the English averages with 87 wickets for a mere 11.01 runs apiece.

It was said that had he been an Englishman, 'Bart' King would have been a permanent member of the national team. Indeed, serious efforts were made to recruit him for an English county, reputedly with the inducement of a rich widow's hand in marriage.

One strange aspect of King's skill much puzzled a famous novelist – not, as it happens, Sir Arthur Conan Doyle, who proved the problem of King's late swing to be 'elementary', with an innings of 41 not out against the Philadelphians at Lord's, but the late C.P. Snow. The mystery that Snow investigated in a 1971 *Cricketer* was why it took so long for King to find imitators on this side of the Atlantic.

It's rather odd, and something of a reproach to cricket intelligence that English bowlers didn't latch on to his example. There were of course inswing bowlers before and just after the First World War, W.T. Greswall and Jaques of Hampshire and Fred Root. But it remains a mystery that the full rigour of the modern game didn't set in until so late.

C.P. Snow went on to lament the fact that swing had ever been invented, thinking no doubt of many dour encounters under favouring cloud which in the 1950s and 1960s were to see the batsman rendered strokeless against the seaming ball.

As far as can be ascertained, most pace bowlers of King's day sought to obtain movement off the wicket, rather than in the air, with cutters or spin. A photograph of the great S.F. Barnes, for instance, shows that he is gripping the ball *across* the seam. Harder work, certainly, than holding the seam up and letting shine and atmosphere do the rest, which perhaps explains why it was only with the arrival of the age of labour-saving devices that the message from America finally got through.

THE BOY'S OWN PAPER   Emrik & Binger, Chromolith. 15 Holborn Viaduct. [56 PATERNOSTER ROW.E.C. LONDON.

The high tide of America's cricket glory. The Gentlemen of Philadelphia rank with the Australians in 1884.

'Bart' King lived long enough to see his innovation become standard practice; a regular visitor to England, he died in 1965 at the ripe old age of ninety-two. We do not know what he thought of his latter-day disciples, but 'the compleat angler' must have been pleased to note that his 1908 average was not improved upon for fifty years – and then only by another king of swing, the vastly under-selected England player Les Jackson from Derbyshire.

ABDUL'S EASTERN MAGIC

The last time a leg-spin bowler was picked to play for England was the season of 1971 when Robin Hobbs of Essex and later Glamorgan appeared in the Third Test *v* Pakistan at Headingley. The fact that Hobbs took no wickets (though he was limited to only four overs in Pakistan's second innings) must have confirmed the selectors in the view that leg-spin bowling is a luxury that modern cricket can afford to do without. Certainly, by 1982 when Imran Khan led Pakistan on a

S.F. Barnes. Pace with a spin
action (see page 16).

Pakistan's Abdul Qadir in a sunny
mood.

short England tour, there was not a full-time leg-spinner and googly bowler to be found in the counties. The breed of B.J.T. Bosanquet was extinct.

However, such was not the case on the Indian sub-continent. I have a photograph of the Pakistanis in England in 1982. Standing at the extreme right of the back row is a young man of medium height whose presence in the party would appear to be dimmed by the all-star line-up in front of him which includes the likes of Majid and Imran Khan, Zaheer Abbas and Sarfraz Nawaz. Yet from today's angle it looks probable that the fame and influence of this back-row team member will endure longer than those of any of the men in the foreground.

Abdul Qadir did not quite sweep all before him in 1982. Nevertheless, he was clearly of the opinion (when is he not?) that he deserved a vastly bigger haul than his respectable ten wickets in three Tests, for as *Wisden* reported, 'the failure of England's batsmen to distinguish Abdul Qadir's googly from his leg-break meant that . . . he was forever rapping the pads and letting forth an impassioned appeal.' *Wisden* goes on to record some ominous rumblings regarding umpiring decisions, which will not be discussed at this point. Yet it may be that Qadir is always destined to be associated with umpiring controversy, if only because his subtlety of spin must pose nearly as many problems for the man in the white coat as it does for the batsman. Added to this, we have in Abdul Qadir the nearly unique phenomenon of a slow man with the aggressive temperament of a fast bowler.

Between 1982 and his 1987 *annus mirabilis*, Qadir enjoyed days of both spectacular success and more modest achievement, though it is doubtful whether any batsman has been relieved to see the ball tossed into his restless hands. Certainly Qadir was fortunate in his first captain, Imran Khan, who championed his genius as resolutely as did P.F. Warner that of Bosanquet, even to the extent of insisting on his inclusion in the team for the First Test at Old Trafford in 1987, despite the fact that due to family problems he was plainly short of practice. A nervier captain, and nervous captains have often been the downfall of leg-break bowlers, might have settled for the safer option of more pace.

There have been days, when the clouds are low and the wicket is not responsive, when Abdul Qadir can look almost like an ordinary bowler. In the Bicentenary Match at Lord's in 1987, for instance, where he was pitted against the world's finest batsmen, he seemed to be wheeling away as benevolently as Eric Hollies of Warwickshire or 'Rolly' Jenkins of Worcestershire in the bland summers of the 1950s. But with the sun on his back, the damp out of his finger joints and an English helmet in his sights, Abdul Qadir can be a series winner all on his own. Much was made of the friendly encouragement and support he seemed to receive from local umpires in the notorious England–Pakistan series in the last

'Forever rapping the pads and letting forth an impassioned appeal.' Here David Gower is given out in the First Test, Pakistan *v* England, Karachi, 1984.

The action that offers few clues to the batsman. Abdul Qadir sends down another teaser during the 1987 World Cup.

Abdul Qadir on the attack with an England helmet in his sights, Edgbaston, 1982.

quarter of 1987. Yet the fact remains that five years after his arrival on the Test scene, no English batsman can read him.

Unlike the earlier googly men who could betray their secret weapon with a change of arm angle or a more open-chested delivery, Qadir's action is practically identical for his leg-break, googly and top-spinner. And it's not only the batsman who can be mystified. As Norman Harris wrote in the *Sunday Times* during the Lahore Test:

> Graham Gooch was playing the top-spinner from off the pitch in England's first innings, but had his off stump removed before he could half complete the stroke. It was a supreme moment for any leg-spinner. But don't blame Gooch. Even the wicketkeeper was shaping to take a leg-break.

A clue to Abdul's Eastern magic lies in a first 'trigger finger' which, rather than the wrist, dictates the direction of the spin. Qadir's deceptive action and the batsman's hesitant reaction surely establish him as one of the great innovative bowlers, albeit in the Bosanquet tradition. At this point it is hard to determine what his influence on batsmanship will be, other than making disappointing reading of leading players' averages. Yet if the history of cricket is any guide, an effective method of counter-attack will sooner or later be developed.

In the wider context, Abdul Qadir's great contribution to cricket may be to force the world's selectors to review their policy of massive investment in pace and defensive off-spin. Already we can detect the influence of Abdul Qadir behind the emergent Test career of Australia's leg-spinner, Peter Sleep, though he is still rarely selected for one-day internationals. If more 'mystery spinners' are to be the future trend in Test selection, Abdul Qadir will be due a hearty vote of thanks. For, even in the gloom of England's commentary box during the last series with Pakistan in 1987, every commentator felt bound to admit that there is no better spectacle than that of an ace spinner weaving his magic.

2
CASTING A GIANT SHADOW

Cricket has been altered by laws and administrators, variations of climate, new technology, and a reasonable number of fair but not great players whom history has saddled with the responsibility for having changed the course of the game. But there remains a handful of men who through sheer genius and physical prowess have cast a longer shadow across the game than any number of legislators.

CRICKET'S FATHER FIGURE

The first of these men is a national myth, as well as an outstanding Gloucestershire and England cricketer – a kind of summer Santa Claus who scattered runs, records and good cheer through the Victorian seasons and was, no doubt, prayed to by Victorian children. The man in question is, of course, William Gilbert Grace.

The father figure of cricket was not, as it happened, a great thinker about the game, although as a captain he had an uncanny instinct for a batsman's vulnerable points. According to some reports, he was not even a thrilling stroke-maker. However, he possessed, apart from an impressive physique and a remarkably good eye, one completely novel idea, which was to go on putting bat to ball from start of play until stumps. As a result, Grace set up an extraordinary number of records and in the process made news and thousands of new friends for cricket.

This is not a book of records, but some of Grace's 'firsts' must be noted if only to convey the stature of the man.
Many benefits flowed from Grace's affection for the crease, not least amongst which was a system of batting which could take virtually every type of bowling in its stride. Until his appearance in first-class cricket in 1865, batting had been a specialist's business – forward and backward men, hard hitters and dedicated blockers. Grace's principle was to plant the right foot firmly behind the crease and use the left as a direction-finder for run-scoring all round the clock, 'like a kind of rotating oak tree' I believe I've written elsewhere.

W.G.'s career lasted long enough to see off all manner of bowling fashions – the steady, medium pace of the Alfred Shaw school, the novel speed of the Australian fast bowlers of the 1880s, and the 'off theorists', Attewell and Co., who pegged away with varying speed and length outside the off stump with the aim of producing catches for a packed off-side field (though here, as we shall see, it was his talented elder brother, E.M. Grace, who pointed the way).

Of course, there was another side to the coin which was, not to put too fine a point on it, the good doctor's reluctance to depart from the crease unless his wicket was demonstrably wrecked. The best-known story concerning his disinclination to 'walk' also explains the economics of cricket in Grace's time – 'They came to see me bat, not you bowl.' For what could not be disputed was that on his way to all those astonishing records, W.G. had made cricket big business.

Even at the flipping of the coin, Grace could be a gamesman. 'The

'W.G.'s career lasted long enough to see off all manner of bowling fashions.'

1871	First to make 2000 runs in a season.
1873	First man to do the 'double' (1000 runs, 100 wickets). First to score a century before lunch.
1876	Set up the highest score hitherto in first-class cricket: 344 runs.
1895	At the age of forty-six, first to score 1000 runs in May.

Lady!', he would call, when tossing up with an opposing skipper. Either way he stood to be the winner, with the Queen for heads and Britannia for tails.

To read some of his younger contemporaries, one may get the impression of a surprisingly limited batsman in modern terms. Apparently he lacked the majestic cover-drive of the MacLaren generation. According to the Hon. Edward Lyttelton he was incapable of the wristy cut, offering instead a 'similar blow'. However, Lyttelton admits that one such 'similar blow' from the doctor 'once struck the horny hand of [Lancashire's] Barlow fielding at point and raced without noticeable deflection to the boundary'. Again it seems that Ranji's deft leg-glances were no part of the great man's armoury, and Neville Cardus suggests that his technique was suspect against googly bowling.

However, none of these quibbles erases a single run from those monumental records. Certainly no one has ever attempted to deny the doctor's unrivalled appetite for batting – and bowling for that matter; only towards the end of his career did he tend to count himself out of his team's strike force. Indeed, it is surely the man's titanic energy that primarily accounts for his mighty impact on the game.

Opposite: Father figure of an age – W.G. Grace.

W.G. GRACE: RUNS AND WICKETS IN ALL CLASSES OF CRICKET

Year	First-class Runs	First-class Wickets	Minor matches Runs	Minor matches Wickets	Year	First-class Runs	First-class Wickets	Minor matches Runs	Minor matches Wickets
1857	—	—	4	0	1886	1846	122	233	31
1858	—	—	17	0	1887	2062	97	409	45
1859	—	—	12	0	1888	1886	93	138	33
1860	—	—	82	0	1889	1396	44	978	96
1861	—	—	102	3	1890	1476	61	218	20
1862	—	—	298	22	1891	771	58	530	49
1863	—	—	673	70	1891/2	448	5	555	50
1864	—	—	1189	122	1892	1055	31	53	17
1865	197	20	1972	175	1893	1609	22	654	36
1866	581	31	1583	198	1894	1293	29	613	77
1867	154	39	654	71	1895	2346	16	236	5
1868	625	49	1200	86	1896	2135	52	261	14
1869	1320	73	1026	81	1897	1532	56	343	20
1870	1808	50	1452	86	1898	1513	36	272	13
1871	2739	79	1074	106	1899	515	20	1459	82
1872	1561	68	1008	108	1900	1277	32	1398	130
1873	2139	106	925	123	1901	1007	51	2011	111
1873/4 (Australia)			866	66	1902	1187	46	1458	115
1874	1664	140	1187	130	1903	593	10	1254	60
1875	1498	191	1293	217	1904	637	21	944	111
1876	2622	129	1268	88	1905	250	7	1118	123
1877	1474	179	997	211	1906	241	13	876	68
1878	1151	152	658	184	1907	19	—	1040	104
1879	993	113	35	19	1908	40	—	684	116
1880	951	84	1150	133	1909	—	—	41	1
1881	917	57	1360	172	1910	—	—	418	21
1882	975	101	1404	171	1911	—	—	369	30
1883	1352	94	1096	100	1912	—	—	139	3
1884	1361	82	703	56	1913	—	—	247	6
1885	1688	117	494	57	1914	—	—	205	4

As the above records amply illustrate, the father figure of English cricket was a prolific run-scorer, and his ebullient personality at the crease attracted many new supporters to the game.

Source: *W.G. Grace*, by Bernard Darwin, Duckworth, 1978.

In one of his first matches (England *v* Surrey at The Oval, where he scored 224 not out) the eighteen-year-old Grace was given leave from the field to compete in the quarter-mile hurdle at the Crystal Palace, which he won by a handsome margin. W.G. did not continue with his athletics career, but he did continue to lead his life at a cracking pace. His exertions on the field in no way prevented him from being the life and soul of the elegant parties that were the essence of cricketing life in this period.

It seems that Grace would go almost anywhere for a game of cricket. He once turned up in a club match under the alias of 'Mr Green', and his true identity was discovered only when he had scored a century. But perhaps the most revealing of all the W.G. anecdotes is the amazing story of the fishes (although not loaves in this case!). Sitting up late one night over a glass or two with his old friend William Murdoch of Australia and Sussex, Grace took it into his head to bet five gold sovereigns that his pal, who was playing in a county match the following day, would score fewer runs than he could catch fish. Grace lumbered out of bed at three in the morning and by supper-time was tottering home with a massive haul of precisely 100 roach and other assorted river fish, only to find that Murdoch had scored 103.

W.G. Grace was a master competitor who, while others tired or lost concentration, carried on batting until he had converted the game of cricket into a national obsession. He died in October 1915.

BRADMAN AND THE TRIUMPH OF WILLPOWER

Sir Donald Bradman (born 1908 and still going strong) was the greatest cricketing phenomenon after Grace, many of whose records he soon diminished. Like Grace, he was responsible for bringing the crowds flocking to cricket and causing millions more bosoms to swell with national pride – Australian pride in this case, of course. Yet the two men could not have been less alike. While Grace towered over his team-mates, Bradman was hardly noticeable when the Australians took the field – his was the bulky green cap bobbing along at around shoulder level to men such as Woodfull, Brown, Fingleton and O'Reilly. Unlike the gregarious doctor, there was little after-hours socializing for the Don. He would hurry home to his family or sit alone in his hotel bedroom contemplating the century or two he *knew* he would score the next day. This brings us to the crucial differences between the men: while Grace's greatest strength had been his natural prowess, Bradman's was his willpower.

There is an element of the 'rags to riches' story in Bradman's early life which ideally qualified him to be a hero of the Depression years of the 1930s. Again, his brilliant career coincided with an explosion in the entertainment industry, which came about as a result of radio, the 'talkies', and millions of people the world over looking for an escape from the bleak times. The emerging technology ensured that Bradman's records were as massive in their impact as those of Bing Crosby.

In six Tests the young Donald had already taken five centuries off England (if his double century in the previous Lord's Test is included) by the time he came to Headingley in 1930. The England team could have been excused for thinking that he was due for a failure. After all, up to this point there had been no such thing as an infallible batsman. Besides, Harold Larwood, England's best speed bowler, was fully fit again. In the event, it transpired that at Lord's Bradman had merely been tuning up for another unique achievement. *The Cricketer* reported glumly, 'Shortly after he had passed his 200 Bradman made his first poor stroke, mis-hitting a ball from Tyldesley just out of Tate's reach at mid-on.'

At the Third Test at Headingley, Australia won the toss and decided to bat on a fine, if slightly chilly, July morning. Things started

A cigarette card artist depicts the Bradman cut. The real thing would have been more decisive.

Donald G. Bradman at the start
of a forward stroke.

Donald Bradman waves to the
Leeds crowds as he passes R.E.
Foster's 287 record for the highest
score in Test cricket.

promisingly for England when Jackson was caught by Larwood off
Tate with only two runs on the board. Yet this brought Bradman to the
wicket in good time to put up a century (105) by lunch. Hammond and
Geary managed to apply a steadying influence after lunch, the former
capturing Woodfull's wicket for 50. But the return of Larwood and
Tate with the new ball presented Bradman with the pace he needed to
recapture his momentum. By the tea interval he was 220 not out. At two
minutes past six he swept past R.E. Foster's 287 record for Anglo-
Australian Tests in five and a half hours, compared with Foster's seven

hours and twenty minutes. At precisely 6.20 Bradman became the only man to score 300 in a day in Test cricket, which he remains to this day.

The press pictures of this pulverizing and vastly influential knock tended to show two slips still eagerly awaiting a miscue from the man who rarely made a mistake, while England's captain and gallant close-fielder, A.P.F. Chapman, is seldom out of frame.

'Why didn't you close up the game and bowl on his leg stump to a leg-trap?', a young Test player asked Maurice Tate many years later.

'It never occurred to me,' confessed the great Sussex bowler. 'It never occurred to any of us. In those days you aimed to get them out with every ball.'

It *did* seem to have occurred to the selectors, however. Bradman's 300 runs in a day was to have the immediate result of costing Chapman his job. In the longer term it would have the grim effect of introducing containment into Test cricket, by one means or another. One method was Bodyline, and we shall shortly look at the repercussions that this caused. There can be no doubt that Bradman had a demoralizing effect on the bowling craft in the 1930s, both in England and Australia, and not a few Australian and state batsmen felt cheated of fame and fortune as they waited, padded up in the pavilion, for some quirk of fate to

Bradman hits out in yet another Test of mortal achievement.

remove the master innings builder from the middle.

Again, many critics, Neville Cardus amongst them, suggested that the inevitable success of a Bradman innings (at least before Bodyline) robbed it of appeal and savour. Much the same would later be said of Geoffrey Boycott, although perhaps with more justification in view of the Yorkshireman's radically slower scoring rate. All the same, one suspects there is something in the popular heart that loves a massive run-compiler, recognizing in him a man who is winning glory for humankind in the ultimate test of mortal achievement.

SIR DONALD BRADMAN: FIRST-CLASS CAREER STATISTICS

	Matches	Inns	NO	Runs	HS	Aver.	100s	50s	Ct
1927/8	5	10	1	416	134*	46.22	2	1	0
1928/9	13	24	6	1690	340*	93.88	7	5	3
1929/30	11	16	2	1586	452*	113.28	5	4	4
1930	27	36	6	2960	334	98.66	10	5	12
1930/1	12	18	0	1422	258	79.00	5	4	7
1931/2	10	13	1	1403	299*	116.91	7	0	5
1932/3	11	21	2	1171	238	61.63	3	7	6
1933/4	7	11	2	1192	253	132.44	5	4	4
1934	22	27	3	2020	304	84.16	7	6	9
1935/6	8	9	0	1173	369	130.33	4	1	7
1936/7	12	19	1	1552	270	86.22	6	2	10
1937/8	12	18	2	1437	246	89.81	7	5	13†
1938	20	26	5	2429	278	115.66	13	5	8
1938/9	7	7	1	919	225	153.16	6	0	3
1939/40	9	15	3	1475	267	122.91	5	4	11
1940/1	2	4	0	18	12	4.50	0	0	0
1945/6	2	3	1	232	112	116.00	1	2	1
1946/7	9	14	1	1032	234	79.38	4	4	4
1947/8	9	12	2	1296	201	129.60	8	1	9
1948	23	31	4	2428	187	89.92	11	8	11
1948/9	3	4	0	216	123	54.00	1	1	3
	234	338	43	28,067	452*	95.14	117	69	131†

* Not Out.
† Also one stumping in 1937/8.
Of his 131 catches, four were made as wicket-keeper. He made one further catch in first-class cricket while fielding as substitute in the Second Test at Sydney in 1928–9.

The Don's cricketing statistics speak for themselves. Bradman's phenomenal averages, unmatched to this day, made him Australia's hero of the 1930s and the scourge of the England bowlers.

Source: *Sir Donald Bradman (A Biography)*, by Irving Rosenwater, B.T. Batsford, 1978.

HOBBS AND HAMMOND

It's not as easy as it might seem to find a 'third man' to join the Grace and Bradman duo, although there is no shortage of candidates. The MCC has no doubts as to his identity: it is Sir Jack Hobbs, who stands alongside the others in the form of a giant blown-up photograph in the Lord's museum.

Certainly, Hobbs stands tall among the all-time greats. He scored more runs and centuries (98 of them after his fortieth birthday) than any other batsman before or after him, and no one, not even Bradman, could compare with him on a rain-affected wicket. Again, as can be seen in Chapter 5 of this section, the Surrey and England opener was to play a crucial part in the development of modern batting methods. Yet somehow Hobbs seems more distant from us than the two other giants; the shadow he casts is perhaps not quite so long. This may be because Hobbs was one example a type of cricketer that has almost completely disappeared, a dedicated professional who was content to serve under nine less gifted or less knowledgeable England captains in Anglo-Australian Tests alone, and only once got to lead England when A.W. Carr had to leave the field with tonsilitis. Hobbs continued quietly scoring his elegant centuries through twenty-six 'golden age' and post-war seasons while flashier personalities came and went. It might be said that he was so dependable that he became a part of the landscape of English cricket between 1905 and 1934 – a halcyon period that has gone forever.

PLAYER'S CIGARETTES

W. R. HAMMOND

W.R. Hammond. England's 'ace card' in the Bradman era.

JACK HOBBS: BATTING PROFILE

	Inns	NO	Runs	100s	50s	Highest Inns	Aver.
1905	54	3	1317	2	4	155	25.82
1906	53	6	1913	4	10	162*	40.70
1907	63	6	2135	4	15	166*	37.45
1907/8 (in Australia)	22	1	876	2	6	115	41.71
1908	53	2	1904	6	7	161	37.33
1909	54	2	2114	6	7	205	40.65
1909/10 (in South Africa)	20	1	1194	3	7	187	62.84
1910	63	3	1982	3	14	133	33.03
1911	60	3	2376	4	13	154*	41.68
1911/12 (in Australia)	18	1	943	3	2	187	55.47
1912	60	6	2042	3	14	111	37.81
1913	57	5	2605	9	12	184	50.09
1913/14 (in South Africa)	22	2	1489	5	8	170	74.45
1914	48	2	2697	11	6	226	58.63
1919	49	6	2594	8	14	205*	60.32
1920	50	2	2827	11	13	215	58.89
1920/1 (in Australia)	19	1	924	4	2	131	51.33
1921	6	2	312	1	1	172*	78.00
1922	46	5	2552	10	9	168	62.24
1923	59	4	2087	5	8	136	37.94
1924	43	7	2094	6	10	211	58.16
1924/5 (in Australia)	17	1	865	3	5	154	54.06
1925	48	5	3024	16	5	266*	70.32
1926	41	3	2949	10	12	316*	77.60
1927	32	1	1641	7	5	150	52.93
1928	38	7	2542	12	10	200*	82.00
1928/9 (in Australia)	18	1	962	2	7	142	56.58
1929	39	5	2263	10	8	204	66.55
1930	43	2	2103	5	14	146*	51.29
1931	49	6	2418	10	7	153	56.23
1932	35	4	1764	5	9	161*	56.90
1933	18	0	1105	6	3	221	61.38
1934	18	1	624	1	4	116	36.70
Totals	1315	106	61,237	197	271	316*	50.65

Once described as a professional who batted like an amateur, Hobbs continued to make elegant and consistent centuries through twenty-six cricket seasons.

Source: *Jack Hobbs, Profile of 'The Master'*, by John Arlott, John Murray and Davis-Poynter, 1981.

Walter Hammond is another contender for 'third man' status in this author's view, if only because of the aura of the man at the crease. In terms of innate authority, Hammond seemed to dwarf all around him, and these usually included figures such as Hutton, Compton and

J.B. Hobbs of Surrey and England.
He stands tall among the all-time
greats.

Edrich. However, Hammond failed sadly in three vital series against Australia. His average is 34.00 against Bradman's 139.14 in the 1930 series, 20.86 against the Australian's 94.75 in the 1934 series, and 21.00 against Bradman's 97.10 in 1946/7. In other words, there were times when the second giant of Gloucestershire was the despair of his fans.

DENIS COMPTON AND

THE SUMMERS THAT SAVED CRICKET

D.C.S. Compton comes below J.B. Hobbs and W.R. Hammond (and one place under W.G. Grace incidentally) in *Wisden's* list of scorers of 'most individual hundreds', which many regard as the most telling measure of a batsman's stature. Nevertheless, in my book he stands a few vital inches above them by virtue of his spectacular services to post-war cricket.

Opposite: Compton (right) and his county colleague Bill Edrich, partners in vintage years for cricket.

England entered the post-war era with a rain-spoiled series against India and a crushing defeat by Australia in the winter of 1946 /7. The public started to look for other heroes on the football field, in speedway and even on the bicycle track. It is significant that when the bitter winter of 1947 brought industry to a standstill and the distraught Labour Government decided to ban mid-week sport, cricket was made the exception to this savage rule on the grounds that it attracted negligible numbers of essential industrial workers. Thus there is, arguably, a slot for Labour Prime Minister Clement Attlee in this volume as the man who made Compton's fabulous 1947 season possible.

The snows finally made way for a gorgeous summer, and almost immediately Denis Compton began to demonstrate what an attraction cricket could be. By mid May his centuries were coming with the regularity of Bradman's. He scored three between the last week of May and the first week in June, including 154 in a Test against South Africa. But this was just the beginning; over the season with his Middlesex partner Edrich, who was also enjoying a vintage year, he would share in no fewer than seven partnerships of over 200.

It has to be admitted that the average county attack in 1947 was not formidable. Most still depended on old war-horses from the 1930s, some still a little stiff in the joints from the long 1939–45 lay-off. Yet at a time of maximum austerity (even bread was rationed), Compton took the fullest advantage of these moderate attacks to put the riches of aggressive batting on show. With savage cuts, pulls and sweeps he destroyed just about every county's attack that season, but it was done with a smile and many a mad dash down the wicket, which at least gave the opposition hope of a run out, though usually it was Compton's partner who was left stranded.

Denis Compton and the famous sweep in action against Worcestershire at Lord's.

Gradually, the turnstiles began to rotate merrily as the crowds flooded back to cricket. Imagine a Test-match crowd for a weekday county match between Middlesex and Essex! But that's my recollection of a Compton run spree in August of that amazing season (though I had

no way of knowing how many of those present were essential industrial workers).

Compton and his Middlesex twin, Bill Edrich, could hardly have hoped to stage a repeat performance in the following season, for it brought Bradman's Australians to England, spearheaded by Lindwall and Miller with a variety of relentlessly hostile bowlers in support. As it happened, they did not disappoint their followers, and Compton in particular was able to prove conclusively that he was a man for all seasons. In place of the haymaker in the sunshine of 1947, the public was given a Horatius at Trent Bridge and a battle hero at Old Trafford where, despite a knock-out blow from Lindwall, he returned to the field to score an epic 145 not out. England went down to another series defeat against Australia, but the public's faith in Compton, and cricket, had been triumphantly sustained.

Dennis Compton was soon afterwards to be plagued by a football injury to his knee, and some of the crowds began to desert the cricket grounds for television and for the sport that had almost crippled Compton. The game itself was to become duller, for a decade at least. But in those two vintage seasons, Denis Compton (never forgetting Bill Edrich) had provided a glimpse of what glorious fun cricket could be, and that was enough to keep the faithful returning to Lord's summer after summer until something approaching those good times arrived again.

BOTHAM TO THE RESCUE

We now move forward thirty years to the season of 1977. It witnesses a satisfactory series for England against Australia, featuring such attractions as the return of Geoff Boycott to Test cricket with an innings of 107, the first three consecutive Test wins for England since 1886, and the first Test appearance of a promising young all-rounder from the West Country named I.T. Botham, who takes an encouraging 5 for 74 in Australia's first innings in the Trent Bridge Test. Nevertheless, a shadow hangs over the game in the shape of Kerry Packer. Almost the

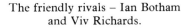

The friendly rivals – Ian Botham and Viv Richards.

entire Australian touring party has been signed for 'World Series Cricket' that winter, and key members of the England team – Greig, Woolmer, Underwood and Knott – have also been recruited. The future of Test cricket, as the world has known it, is seriously in doubt.

Ian Botham has many spectacular achievements to his name, but it's possible that his most outstanding contribution was to ensure the continued popularity of 'official' Tests. One could argue that Botham was lucky in that his astonishing early successes in Tests were earned against Packer-weakened Pakistani and Australian sides. But the point is, surely, that with his joyous batting and aggressive bowling, not to mention those tumbling slip catches, Botham provided a huge element of entertainment value for white-flannelled cricket as opposed to the

Ian Botham strikes another blow for entertainment in cricket. The man close-in is not so amused.

new pyjama brand, and may indeed have contributed to the final abandonment of the alternative experiment. In any case, while no new stars emerged from Packer cricket (and in Tony Greig's case one was effectively extinguished), 'official' Test cricket certainly produced a megastar in Ian Botham.

Statistically Botham is undoubtedly a giant, but his impact on the game has also been immense. He can be credited with bringing 'the roar of the crowd' back to cricket, being of that rare type of player who will cause a spectator to leap into a taxi and shout 'Lord's!' in order to see him bat. And apart from his staggering figures, Botham is the author of one of cricket's truly epic innings, destined to be recalled as long as the game is played.

The scene, of course, is Headingley, 1981. England with 5 down for 105 in their second innings still require 122 to avoid an innings' defeat. Botham's blistering 149 not only obliges Australia to bat again, but inspires England to snatch an incredible 18-run victory. 'The crowd massed in front of the pavilion, cheering their heroes and waving the Union Jacks they were saving for the Royal wedding,' reported John Woodcock of *The Times*. 'The game was a victory for cricket,' he concluded, and added, 'To hear them singing Jerusalem down below you'd think it had revived a nation too!'

VIV RICHARDS FOR LASTING GREATNESS?

The outstanding West Indian batsman before the Second World War was George Headley, who was dubbed the 'Black Bradman'. After the war came the formidable trio of Worrell, Walcott and Weekes, who with scant regard for their distinctive skills were merged as the 'Three Ws'. Viv Richards is unlikely to be remembered as the equivalent of an Australian batsman with a darker skin, or to be grouped together with other gifted players in the West Indies batting line-up. He is a highly individual player, and it is more likely that his name will be used to indicate an era in West Indian cricket.

First, a few statistics. Between January and September 1976 I.V.A. Richards scored 1710 in Tests, beating the record for the highest scoring in a calendar year. Against England in that summer he averaged 118, thus becoming the only man to approach Bradman's amazing 139 average in the 1930 England *v* Australia Tests. Richards is the scorer of the fastest century in one-day internationals, and by the time we go to press he will almost certainly be approaching Bradman's record for number of centuries scored. But more to the point, Richards is a highly charismatic batsman who can send a roar of excited expectation round a cricket ground as he swaggers out to bat.

That self-same swagger can sometimes be this giant's undoing – witness the contemptuous slash that cost him his wicket to Eddie Hemmings in the vital England *v* West Indies encounter during the 1987 World Cup. Consistency is certainly not the hallmark of his style. As early as 1974 there were rumblings down in Somerset concerning Richards' ability to get himself out when the needs of the team required him to stay in. One particular drive into the stratosphere, which was finally gathered by the wicket-keeper after Richards and his partner had crossed twice, was cited as an example of this tendency.

However, from both the bowler's and the crowd's point of view, a Richards innings is the reverse of what the critics found unappealing in a Bradman knock – instead of predictability there is always a chance that a sudden rush of blood to the head will terminate the devastating assault. On the other hand, it is equally possible that he will completely rout the opposition with another blazing century. In other words, Viv Richards is erratically great, perhaps like cricket itself. For this reason alone it's hard to predict how far his shadow will reach into the future.

Opposite: Another certain four from the bat of Viv Richards.

3
THE LAW CREATORS

Many of today's cricket laws and codes (some of them over two hundred years old) can be traced directly back to individuals whose manner or methodology has forced the administrators into legislative action. For example, John Ring of Kent (1758–1800) may not have seen himself as a law-maker; in fact, he would have been outlawed had he not mended his ways. Yet he is responsible for one of the most controversial pieces of legislation in cricket – the vexed lbw law.

LEG BEFORE AND THE THIRD STUMP

Ring was a short man of just 5 foot 5 inches, but he could be a punishing batsman, leg-hits being both his strength and, as we shall see, his weakness. His basic problem was his patron and sponsor, Sir Horace Mann, who expected great things of his protégé and recompensed Ring by results on which he himself would usually have had a handsome wager. As William Beldham, the grand old man of Hambledon, was to recall for the benefit of the Reverend James Pycroft:

> I remember him in one match in Kent. Ring was playing against David Harris. The game was much against him. Sir Horace Mann was cutting about with his stick among the daisies and cheering every run – you would have thought his whole fortune (and he would often bet some hundreds) was staked upon the game; and, as a new man was going in, he went across to Ring and said, 'Ring, carry your bat through and make up all the runs, and I'll give you £10 a year for life.' Well, Ring was out for sixty runs and only three to tie, and four to beat, and the last man made them.

The glittering prizes held out by this demanding patron must have been at the back of John Ring's mind when, in another match for Kent, 'he was shabby enough to get his leg in the way and take advantage of the bowlers'. (Beldham again.) Was it another promise of rich rewards for life that turned John Ring's legs into a defensive wall? In any case, it proved to be the last straw when Ring's partner, Tom Taylor, began to

As with stumps and bats, the shape of scoring has changed over the years. This is the Hambledon version of a scoreboard.

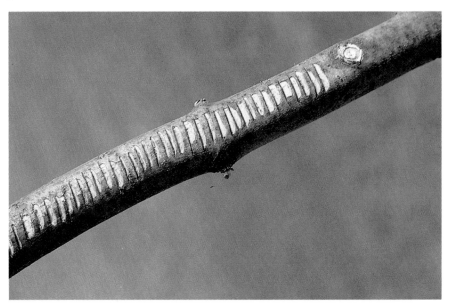

imitate his tactics, and the 'leg before' law was a direct result of this unentertaining fixture.

It must be remembered that the wicket John Ring was putting his leg before was not much higher than a croquet hoop. It measured 22 inches by 6. Moreover, until 1775 it lacked a middle stump. This deficiency finally came to officialdom's attention when, 'five of the Hambledon Club' were playing 'five of All England' at the Artillery Ground. The great Kent underarmer, 'Lumpy' Stevens, was bowling to John Small of the Hambledon Club. Near to despair at seeing that the ball had 'three several times passed between Small's stumps', the bowler appealed to the authorities and was awarded that vital middle stump.

THE END OF SHARP BATTING PRACTICE

It was about this time that new laws were made as to bat width and weight. A crafty character known as White of Ryegate brought a bat to a game which precisely matched the dimension of the wicket. White, an ultra-defensive batsman on the evidence, might never have been dislodged had it not been decreed that thereafter a bat should be no wider than 4½ inches.

The wicket as it was before 'Lumpy' Stevens successfully appealed for a third stump.

Edgar Willsher at the beginning of his controversial career.

At the same time, the ball's weight was limited to no more than $5\frac{3}{4}$ oz. The new law was enforced by means of an iron frame, installed in the Hambledon clubhouse, through which any suspect blade was passed to ensure conformity.

OVERARM BECOMES LEGITIMATE

Now for an incident of immense significance for the game, and also of some personal pathos. Edgar Willsher was an overarm fast bowler, one of John Willes' heirs, who had taken the round-arm revolution to its furthest extreme. Technically Willsher's action was illegal, since existing legislation condemned any delivery above shoulder height. However, there seems to have been a tacit agreement among officials and umpires to turn a blind eye to Willsher and his kind – with one important exception.

Umpire John Lillywhite was a stickler for the rules who also, perversely, happened to be a close personal friend of the Surrey paceman. These two loyalties came into painful conflict when Willsher opened the bowling for Surrey against England, a game of Test-match significance in those days, at The Oval in August 1862. For two overs, friendship seems to have prevailed over the letter of the law. But as Willsher began his third over of fast left-arm leg-breaks, Lillywhite immediately no-balled him, and the next five deliveries received a similar call.

A drama of Faisalabad proportions now ensued. All the Surrey players except her two amateurs marched off the field, and the game was not resumed that evening. Unlike umpire Shakoor Rana, however, Lillywhite was replaced by umpire Street the next day. It was glorious

The man who made a mockery of underarm bowling – C.B. Fry – and friends.

Jardine catches Jack Ryder of Australia off Larwood in a 1928 Test, but his main aim was to frustrate Bradman.

weather, a big crowd was expected and the authorities were presumably unwilling to see the team sitting around reading newspapers or issuing protests. Edgar Willsher was allowed to bowl without further let or hindrance.

John Lillywhite, meanwhile, had succeeded in making his point which was, apparently, that the law was an ass and needed amending. Two years later, it duly was. In fact, this umpiring wrangle ended happily both for cricket and for the damaged relationship. Legitimized at last, Willsher came to realize that, after all, he was indebted to his fastidious friend.

C.B. FRY SATIRE ENDS UNDERARM BOWLING

It may be wondered what happened to old-fashioned underarm bowling. The answer is that it continued hand in hand with the new overarm fashion until well into the twentieth century, and is legal to this day. One of England's most successful bowlers on the 1909 tour of South Africa was the Worcestershire 'lobster', G.H. Simpson-Hayward. That the style disappeared from cricket was eventually due to the satirical antics of C.B. Fry in a match against Oxford in 1912. He moved from 180 to 203 against the lob bowler and cricket historian H.S. Altham by swinging his bat between his legs, as if addressing a croquet ball, and the offending style has rarely been seen since.

BRADMAN, JARDINE, WARNER
AND THE INTIMIDATION BAN

Sir Donald Bradman can be said to have had a hand in two important pieces of legislation in the 1930s. In the first instance it was his unbeatable batting, as illustrated by that devastating 300 in a day at Headingley and underlined by the 232 sequel at The Oval, that finally provoked the decision for retributive action. Douglas Jardine was a spectator at Bradman's and Ponsford's combined 342-run feast at The

'Plum' Warner in his playing days.
An unhappy England manager in
the Bodyline series.

Oval in 1930, and is reported to have noticed that both batsmen flinched from Larwood's fastest deliveries. This may seem hard to credit when we read the scorecard – Australia 695 all out, Larwood 1 wicket for 132 runs – but Jardine was there and we, presumably, were not.

So the idea of Bodyline was born and mortal danger came to cricket, perhaps for the first time since fast pace and unprepared pitches had combined to kill a batsman in the summer of 1870. Jardine never admitted that the form of attack he instituted in the Australian summer of 1932/3 was calculated to intimidate. He wrote a book which, to synopsize, argued that Larwood and Voce were so accurate that no physical threat was posed to able batsmen and that, anyway, the Australians were a bunch of whingeing, incompetent cowards. Many Australian batsmen claimed, however, that even if they stood clear of the wicket, the Larwood and Voce rocket force would still seek out a human target.

Later, we will describe the terrible tangle into which the England manager Pelham Warner got himself over the issue. Briefly, he was at first firm in his support of the England captain in the face of the lively protests of the Australian authorities, but later, back in England, he was to undergo a change of heart. There is evidence of some personal ill-feeling between Warner and Jardine, the former believing that the latter had shown scant gratitude for his patronage and trust. Thus Warner joins the chain of instigators (Bradman and Jardine being the first two links) which finally led early in 1934 to the MCC's official sanction against 'the systematic bowling of fast, short-pitched balls at the batsman standing clear of his wicket'. This injunction is still in force, though Brian Close and John Edrich, facing the West Indies at Old Trafford in 1976, have been among recent batsmen who have suspected otherwise.

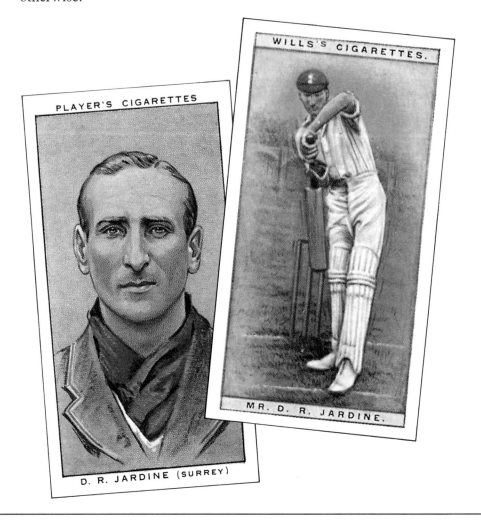

PLAYER'S CIGARETTES

WILLS'S CIGARETTES.

D. R. JARDINE (SURREY)

MR. D. R. JARDINE.

Douglas Jardine of Surrey and
England, a stern face at England's
helm.

BRADMAN AND OTHERS BRING IN

LEGAL RELIEF FOR THE BOWLER

Bradman poses for the camera on his way to his epic 334 at Leeds in 1930. Batting marathons like these hurried the amendment to the lbw rule in 1935.

It would be too flattering, or too unjust, depending on your point of view, to allow Bradman to take all the responsibility for the revised lbw law of 1935. After all, there were plenty of other batsmen around at the time who were able and willing to demonstrate the mastery of bat over ball. One example was Bradman's team-mate Bill Ponsford, the only man to make two scores of over 400. Another was England's Walter Hammond, an imperious demolisher of county bowling, though he occasionally faltered in Tests. And there were also Hendren and Sutcliffe, and the recently retired J.B. Hobbs, who had made bowlers miserable to the last. All the same, one suspects that it was Bradman, the man who seldom risked a shot in the air when he could be sure of a boundary along the grass, who loomed largest in the legislators' minds when they formulated what they hoped would prove an attractive incentive to bowlers to stick at it.

The 1935 amendment made it possible for an umpire to uphold an appeal for a ball pitching outside the off stump if, in his view, it was destined to move in and hit a stump. No such flexibility was permitted on the leg side, however. As a result, the new legislation was to have the effect of hastening the decline of the leg-spinner.

Yorkshire's Hedley Verity was to foresee another negative aspect of the new law: 'As bowlers adapt themselves to the altered rule, accurately bowled in-swing must make off-side strokes, particularly the cover-drive, even more difficult and dangerous to execute.'

In retrospect, it can be argued that while the new law may have given much-needed encouragement to bowlers, it also produced a particularly negative type of attack.

THE LAST OF THE LIGHT APPEALERS

Sidney Barnes of Australia and New South Wales is memorable as a gifted batsman with a sense of humour that was not always appreciated by either the authorities or the crowds. He once took guard with a toy bat in an important testimonial match, and at another, appearing as twelfth man on this occasion, he came on to the field at refreshment time in a butler's outfit dispensing cigars and deodorants and performing other party tricks, for which performance he was jeered from the field.

Barnes is also in the record books as the scorer of the slowest double-century in Anglo-Australian Tests, and it was during this marathon that he was successful in bringing about a fundamental change in the legislation regarding bad light. Up until then, it had been the batsman's privilege to 'appeal against the light', a practice from which many nervous night watchmen had benefited over the years. Barnes effectively removed this privilege on the evening of 14 December 1946.

The crowd had already been robbed through thunder and a string of earlier Barnes appeals of over three hours' play. Now, in fitful sunlight, Barnes further delayed play with an unprecedented five consecutive appeals against the light conditions, the last being reluctantly accepted by the umpires to the chagrin of the crowd. The position was desperate (Sidney Barnes later claimed in his no-punches-pulled autobiography). Australia had already lost opener Arthur Morris cheaply and a further wicket could have put the Poms in the driving seat. (In fact, Hammond's England team, already badly beaten at Brisbane, were to lose this Test by an innings, Barnes and Bradman scoring 234 apiece).

Nowadays, as a result of S.G. Barnes' appealing qualities, the light is 'offered' by the umpires, to use the quaint official phrase. On occasions, as we watch those long mid-wicket conferences with brandished light meters and agonized looks at the skies, we may wonder if any practical gain has been achieved.

S.G. Barnes of Australia, in close-up (above) and at the wicket for Australia *v* MCC in 1948. No sighting problems here!

GORDON RORKE AND THE FRONT-FOOT LAW

Around the late 1950s, it looked as if cricket was about to witness another bowling revolution. Just as in the 1860s umpires and official-dom had turned a blind eye to the overarm style of Willsher and others preparatory to legal approval, it seemed that the bowler whose arm was not quite straight, and even decidedly bent, was about to receive the law-makers' blessing. The pessimists believed that cricket was on the verge of being rudely propelled into a kind of 'baseball era'.

We know that Sir Pelham Warner (it is truly amazing how often his name crops up in the history of twentieth-century cricket) had warned umpire Chester that he would get no support for no-balling the South African 'pitcher' Cuan McCarthy in the Tests of 1951. Presumably, Warner was anxious not to spoil what promised to be an agreeable series against England's then favourite antagonist. Yet a wink can be as good as a nod in Test cricket, as in any other type of combat, and soon, international elevens would begin to include bowlers who could slip one through a little faster than the man who obeyed the old windmill principle.

Ian Meckiff. He 'hurled out' England in the second Melbourne Test.

Meanwhile, another disturbing trend was beginning to manifest itself – drag. The camera showed that several of the front runners in international fast bowling, such as Lindwall and Tyson, were putting down balls with such momentum that in the act of delivery they were 'dragging' the right foot clear of the popping crease. In other words, they were bowling no-balls at a speed difficult for umpires to detect. This tendency might have gone unchecked if it had been confined to orthodox fast bowlers; but with the emergence of the 'chucker-dragger', it became increasingly hard to look the other way. Most countries were guilty of taking advantage of the law's laxity, and the javelin-throwing action of the West Indies' Charlie Griffith was never to be restrained. For the moment, however, it was the Australians who strayed furthest from the path of orthodoxy. In the 1958/9 series against England they threw into the attack two bowlers who would surely have made Sir Pelham Warner's grey hairs stand on end – Ian Meckiff and Gordon Rorke. The dual transgressions of the bent elbow and drag over the crease were blatantly visible with these two bowlers, the technical explanation being that a fast man who skips the conventional preliminaries of a straight-arm action is more likely to find himself yards down the wicket in the act of delivery.

Meckiff alone might not have forced the ultimate decision to legislate, even though E.M. Wellings was to report that he had 'hurled out' six Englishmen for 38 in the Second Melbourne Test. After all, the reporter was English and could be expected to cry 'foul play'. But now, for reasons best known to the selectors, it was decided to double Australia's investment in controversial assault. With England already two down in the series, they picked Gordon Rorke, an even more radical 'storm-and-drag' man.

As an individual, Gordon Rorke was a friendly giant (6 ft 5 in) with a remarkably healthy appetite. A team-mate was to quip, 'Gordon has gone off his food!' when he limited himself to three eggs and three steaks at a pre-Test Breakfast. However, as a bowler he was a 'honey of a chucker', to quote Brian Chapman of the *Daily Mirror*. Besides, his square-chested action took him far into 'Tom Tiddler's ground'. 'You found he was practically landing at your feet,' said Tom Graveney.

Rorke was able to content himself with 8 wickets for 20.62 in the last two Tests of the series. In the end, his career was to end sadly through no fault of the legislators. He contracted hepatitis on a subsequent tour of India and Pakistan and faded from first-class cricket for health reasons.

The 1958–9 tour of Australia was far from being Peter May's finest

Gordon Rorke. In his action and footwork he strayed far from the path of orthodoxy.

hour, yet the England captain maintained a laudable stiff upper lip in regard to the new sling-and-drag weapon. Meanwhile, Australia's leading administrator, Sir Donald Bradman, saw nothing wrong with a series that had given Australia a 4–0 victory – a fitting revenge, any Australian was entitled to feel, after England's 1956 triumph won on pitches that markedly favoured Laker's spin.

Then Bradman was shown slow-motion film which graphically illustrated the technical heresies inherent in the new-style Australian strike weapon. To his considerable credit, he now moved ruthlessly to eliminate the chucking dragger from Australian Test sides, a policy which was to have its just reward when the straight arms of Benaud and Davidson proved sufficient to win the Ashes series of 1961 in England. In the interim, the decisive Don seems to have steeled England's wavering administrators. At Lord's in June 1960 the South African chucker Griffin was repeatedly no-balled, with tragic results for his own career but with crucial long-term benefits for cricket.

As for drag, it was now rigorously curtailed by the new front-foot law, unpopular with all fast men but precise in its insistence that 'some part of the foot whether grounded or raised must be behind the popping crease at the moment of delivery'. The law was always clear about throwing: 'The ball must be bowled, not thrown.' Henceforward, thanks to Rorke and Co., it was to be more rigorously enforced.

4
THE ALL-ROUND
INFLUENCE

There are people, not all of them elderly, who find much to fault in the modern game. Yet when you look around the Test-playing nations, you see that it has one great asset that previous eras lacked, and that is the presence in most international sides of a hard-hitting, pacey all-rounder of star quality. England (it is to be hoped) still has Ian Botham; New Zealand has Richard Hadlee; India has Kapil Dev; and Pakistan has been fortunate to re-acquire the services of Imran Khan. All these men have made prodigious contributions to the health and popularity of cricket in their respective countries, as well as to their own international success.

THE HADLEE EFFECT

Take Richard Hadlee. Until he captured 10 wickets for 100 against England in Wellington in February 1978, New Zealand had had no victory over a span of forty-nine years of Tests against England, and precious few against other Test nations. Richard's father, Walter Hadlee, was considered to have done exceptionally well to hold England to a draw in four three-day Test matches in 1949.

'The Hadlee effect' retards another England young hopeful. Martyn Moxon is out lbw in the First Test, England *v* New Zealand, 1986.

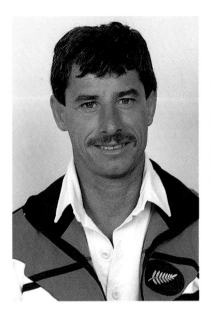

Richard Hadlee. Will he or Botham be the world's top wicket taker?

It cannot be entirely by chance that the younger Hadlee's career has coincided with New Zealand's first Test triumph in England and an underdog to top-dog transformation which resulted in victory over England in two recent series between the countries and a draw in the most recent. Hadlee is a pioneer of New Zealand Test achievement and, to my mind, there is a pioneering look to the man (perhap's it's the moustache!) as he skims in, bent but super-fit, to fell another English oak. The sharp-angled movement he can achieve, into or away from the bat, has brought Hadlee into contention with Ian Botham's 373 Test wickets in 21 fewer Tests. This mercurial all-rounder has taken New Zealand cricket a long way indeed from the time when it was just a game of relaxation for rugby players in summer.

English crowds have had plenty of opportunity to assess Hadlee's all-round entertainment value, since from 1978 to 1987 he was a leading figure in the revival of Nottinghamshire's fortunes, becoming in 1984 the first player since 1967 to achieve that almost forgotten feat, the 'double', with 117 wickets and 1200 runs in the season. Hadlee would almost certainly have repeated the coup in 1987 (97 wickets, 1111 runs) had he not missed two Championship games through his selection for the MCC Bicentenary Match where, unusually, he took no wicket. Typically, however, Hadlee was soon in the news again. Lucky indeed were those with the leisure to spare to enjoy his sweep to victory against the wilting bowlers of Northamptonshire in the delayed NatWest final of the same season.

KAPIL DEVELOPMENTS

Now consider India's Kapil Dev. India did not have to wait for his arrival to beat England in Tests – or anyone else for that matter. However, their victories were usually based on stern 'heads down' batting methods combined with a generous application of spin, as was the case with India's epic win at The Oval in 1971. Fast bowling played virtually no part in the country's triumphs, or even its disasters. When Geoffrey Boycott took leave of Test cricket for three years, following a cheap dismissal by the ultra medium-pacer E.D. Solkar in the First Test against India in 1974, he was widely suspected of not trying. To many, it seemed inconceivable that a batsman of his calibre could be removed for six runs by an Indian opening bowler. But Kapil Dev soon put paid to that theory.

In the summer of 1979, spectators were treated to the rare spectacle of English batsmen ducking and weaving before an Indian opening attack. The new ball was in the hands of two youngsters of far from sedate pace. Their names were K.D. Ghavri and a certain Kapil Dev.

Kapil became the leading Indian wicket-taker in this series. Like Botham, who had come on to the Test scene a couple of years earlier, he would take a little longer to warm up with the bat. But when he did turn on the heat, it was blistering: a century off 83 balls against England in 1982; 89 in 77 minutes and 97 in 102 minutes versus England on their home grounds in the same year. Yet it is the attitude of the man, rather than the figures, that has had such a radical impact on Indian cricket. Who could have imagined, back in the days of the *ancien régime* in the 1970s, that India would discover the aggressive capability to win the World Cup, which is exactly what they did under Dev's leadership on a memorable afternoon at Lord's in 1983.

Kapil Dev's brand of leadership is, in itself, a novelty for India, being characterized by combativeness and willingness to take risks in contrast to the more reflective styles of captains such as V.M. Merchant, Wadekar and Sunil Gavaskar. In the past decade the crown has been passed to and fro between Gavaskar, a formidable competitor in the traditional genteel mould, and the adventure-loving Dev, a boy (at least

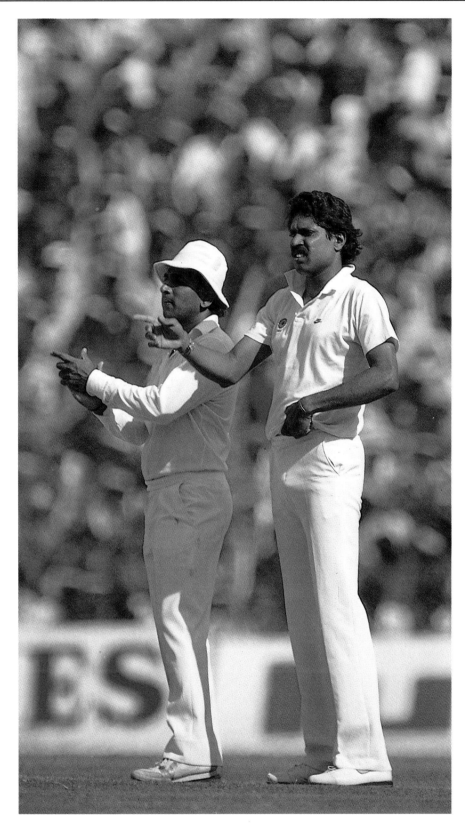

The new face of Indian cricket, the mercurial all-rounder Kapil Dev.

Two men of differing philosophies: Kapil Dev and Sunil Gavaskar compare notes during a one-day international against England at Bangalore in 1985.

at heart) from the provinces, namely the Punjab.

The two men's differing philosophies came notably into conflict during the Delhi Test in the 1984/5 series against England. 'The match is safe, I'm going to have a slog,' Dev told a demurring Sunil Gavasakar, who happened in that series to be the man in the driving seat. In this case, Kapil Dev was proved wrong. His early dismissal by England was soon followed by the sack from the Indian team. Of course he was soon back, and it looks as if the new dynamism represented by Kapil Dev has arrived in Indian cricket to stay.

More action from Kapil Dev.

THE IMRAN INFLUENCE

The impact of Imran Khan on his country's cricket has been similar to that of Kapil Dev on India, only perhaps further-reaching. Before his emergence, Pakistan had produced a number of world-class batsmen and rather fewer bowlers of similar calibre, but no one, even including Asif Iqbal, who combined the two skills as dynamically as this Pathan aristocrat.

Pakistan's famous victory over England in 1954 actually proved to be something of a false dawn. England exacted a terrible revenge in the five-match series of 1962, and there were murmurs in *The Cricketer* to the effect that the Pakistan authorities would be well advised to ask for shorter tours in future. For some years the typical pattern of a Test between the two countries was an enormous England total followed by a heroic, if somewhat fatiguing, rearguard action by the young prodigy Hanif Mohammad or one of his many talented relatives, leading, as often as not, to a draw.

Like Kapil Dev in India, Imran represents a totally new kind of force in Pakistan cricket, a player with the ability rapidly to redeem a desperate situation with the bat and to set up winning opportunities with the ball. And in this respect, his winning influence on his country's fortunes can be compared to Richard Hadlee's on those of New Zealand.

Imran's path to all-round eminence was more difficult than Kapil Dev's. He was selected too early for his country, at the age of eighteen for the 1971 tour of England, and made no impact whatsoever in his single Test appearance. He went back to school, literally, and then, still

Imran Khan, a major influence on the development of Pakistani cricket.

Another England batsman bows to the inevitable – another Test wicket for Imran Khan.

dissatisfied with his all-round performance, moved on to other cricket schools such as Oxford, Worcestershire, Sussex, and finally Packer cricket. Imran provides a rare testimonial to this much-maligned 'circus' by insisting that the time he spent with 'World Series Cricket' was decisive in making him a complete bowler. He expresses his particular indebtedness to South Africa and Gloucestershire player Mike Procter for advice on his run-up, and to John Snow of Sussex and England for his out-swinging secrets.

Thus, many influential experiences back this superb all-rounder in his approach to the crease. Though his roots in Pakistani cricket are deep (he is a cousin of Javed Burki and the great Majid Khan), Imran has a cosmopolitan air and attitude which have ideally qualified him to lead his country out of an introspective past into a triumphant present, and after the mean squabbles of Faisalabad, it is not surprising that he was recalled, almost on bended knee, to bring his inspiring all-round influence back to Pakistani cricket.

The Imran action – with acknowledgements to 'World Series' cricket, Mike Procter and John Snow.

REVERSING THE SPECIALIZATION TREND

Mike Procter, who counselled Imran Khan on his run-up, was perhaps the first of the modern, dynamic all-rounders. Here was a man who, though sadly and severely rationed in his Test appearances, could lift an everyday county match into exalted cricket, as for example when he followed an unbeaten century against Worcestershire at Cheltenham with three wickets in four balls, or, again, when he demolished Glamorgan with 152 in 140 minutes. So where did Mike Procter learn this all-round aggression?

Paradoxically, cricket was becoming an increasingly specialist game before these five men (including Ian Botham, of course) burst upon the scene. This is not to say there weren't notable exceptions to the rule. Sir Garfield Sobers is one mighty example, being not only one of the great post-war bats, but also a man of amazing versatility in bowling alone. Again, Richie Benaud won crucial Test matches as a hard-hitting batsman and a leg-spinner of the highest class. Yet the trend was emphatically towards specialization, and had been for some time. Denis Compton for instance had a highly effective 'Chinaman', give or take a few looseners, and was well capable of breaking a menacing stand when called upon; but he seldom was. Ted Dexter and his seamers once tore through the Players' XI with 5 wickets for 8 runs, 'one of the finest feats in the whole series of [Gentlemen v Players] matches'. Yet he was rarely bowled, and did not often put himself on, in Tests. Going back a little further, Walter Hammond was hailed as one of the greatest all-rounders in the game in the early 1930s. Yet when he became an amateur and captain of England in 1938, he tended to leave the bowling to Farnes, Verity and Bowes. Perhaps he had inherited the odd notion that bowling was something a gentleman seldom did.

This tendency may have helped the great players to concentrate on what they did best, but there was a negative aspect from the spectator's point of view. One suspects that the majority of cricket fans (men as well as boys, women as well as girls) identify with an individual player. Indeed, he is probably the magnet that attracts them to the ground. In my own, more youthful, experience I can recall frustrated hours of watching my hero, Hutton, plucking at his flannels preparatory to getting down to fielding at first slip, or watching Denis Compton chatting good-naturedly with the crowd on the deep third-man boundary when, of course, it was the pair of them at the wicket I had come to see. The mercurial all-rounders we have described present the fan with the opportunity to see his hero almost constantly in action.

Or is this an exaggeration of the importance and desirability of the personality cult in cricket? Certainly, back in the golden age, Gilbert Jessop provided practically non-stop rewards for his fans. A *blitzkrieg* of a batsman, and a bowler of dashing pace, he was also a superb fielder at cover-point, worth a trip to Bristol or Cheltenham even when he scored no runs and took no wickets. It would be convenient to call Jessop the father of the type of cricketer we have been examining in this section, but the truth is that he would be more accurately described as the great-grandfather – a picture hanging on a pavilion wall, too far removed in time to have been able to influence Procter, Botham, Hadlee etc.

Mike Procter of Gloucestershire and South Africa, the modern prototype of the dynamic all-rounder.

Two significant exceptions to the specialization rule. Richie Benaud at the crease (directly above) and Sir Garfield Sobers still posing problems in a Test veterans match.

Let's advance another candidate, though again he is easily old enough to be Kapil Dev's grandfather – West Indies' first cricketing knight, Sir Learie Constantine. This author saw Constantine play only once, for The Commonwealth against England at Lord's in 1945, of which more later. The great man was by then in his early forties, but the enthusiasm of his bowling was astonishing to see. He bowled with his cap on, itself unusual for a fast bowler, and Constantine was the most mobile of fast bowlers hitherto observed. With every unpunished delivery he would race down the pitch with the aim of picking up a caught and bowled from the batsman's defensive prod. Hard work for a man on the wrong side of forty!

Constantine's batting was purpose-built to entertain – he had, after all, spent a long spell as the star attraction with Nelson in the Lancashire League. Sir Learie sought, though not always successfully, to deposit the ball in every stand round the boundary's circumference, but his speciality was a hook which had the apparent aim of removing the wicket-keeper's head. The later Constantine was exhilarating to watch. Yet in these mannerisms, and a few more, he gave the impression of being a cricketer of quite another time. One suspects that this was said of him even in his heyday, as he pitted his galvanic talents against the solemn specialists of the 1920s and the 1930s. However, back to the cricket.

THE FATHER FOUND?

The England *v* Dominions match in the Hiroshima summer of 1945 featured one of the brightest all-star international casts assembled at Lord's before the Bicentenary Match of 1987, and it produced a result. England had Hammond, Gimblett, Edrich and Wright, to mention just a few, while the Dominions (far from achieving Commonwealth status at that time) had Constantine, the brilliant New Zealander M.P. Donnelly, and batting one place above him, the man I would identify as the prototype of today's swashbuckling all-rounder.

My first glimpse of Pilot Officer K.R. Miller had been at the recent 'Victory' Test at Lord's. The moment he stepped out of the shadow of

Learie Constantine at a ceremony to mark the independence of Trinidad and Tobago. His batting was purpose-built to entertain.

the pavilion a shout went up such as had never been heard before on a cricket ground. A measure of its intensity was the fact that several MCC members gently shook their heads at the demonstration. Memory suggests that the tall and immensely handsome airman carried his bat at an angle that was itself liable to produce a nod or two. Rather than trailed, it was parallel with the ground, ready for instant action. In just one previous Test appearance, K.R. Miller had taught the Lord's crowd to expect extraordinary happenings. He scored a blazing 118 in this match and bowled a little, too – fast stuff certainly, but a bit erratic and nowhere near as formidable as it was to become by 1948.

The applause was, if anything, even more rapturous as Miller sprang out to bat in the Dominions' second innings. Perhaps the crowd sensed it had an appointment with history. In any case, it was immediately obvious that England's bowlers – they included two leg-spinners – were in for a miserable morning, even though it happened to be a glorious August day. Anyone outside the stands, fumbling for threepence to pay for a scorecard, say, might have fancied that rifle practice was taking place on the field. Watching from a seat in the ground, the reality was Miller swinging two sixes high up into the Mound Stand followed by two tremendous shots, both sixes, straddling the pavilion. I was one of those lucky enough to have a bird's-eye view of these proceedings, a considerate father having obtained seats at the very top of the pavilion. Then Miller took a step down the wicket, and it became a matter first of ducking and then craning the neck back to follow this gargantuan hit. A crash into the guttering and the muffled oaths of a team of disturbed BBC radio commentators announced that Keith Miller had failed to achieve Alfred Trott's total clearance by only a few tiles. Up until then, I had supposed that a cricket match at Lord's was something that happened at a distance, not in one's lap. Miller had brought the game alive for me.

Keith Miller returned in 1948 as a fearsome fast bowler, though always with a friendly pat on the back for the English batsman whose nose he had nearly removed. As a batsman he had to wait for Bradman, Morris, Harvey and the other specialists to have their turn, especially as he had got himself into Bradman's bad books by throwing away his wicket during the systematic destruction of Essex. Overkill was never appealing to this light bomber pilot. However, for two more English seasons he was to carry on demolishing an attack when he was needed. It happened once again that I was obliged to duck a Miller missile when he casually flicked a six into the old Tavern Stand in the 1953 Lord's Test where he weighed in with a hefty 109.

As skipper of New South Wales, Miller gave evidence that he would have been an Australian captain in the Imran Khan or Kapil Dev mould, if we may be permitted to reverse chronology. However, the Australian selectors insisted on opting for specialist conformism rather than all-round competitiveness. The day of the mercurial captain, bowler and batsman had not yet arrived, although more than anyone else, he made it possible. I see, and hear, that Miller six on to the roof of Lord's pavilion as a shot that was to echo around the world and inspire men not yet born to play the *total* game at full throttle.

5
THE STROKE MAKERS

It is time to turn to the story of batting, and, from all the whirling blades that have enhanced the game, to try to identify those that have fundamentally changed the direction of cricket.

As with the evolution of any technology, the history of batting is littered with false starts and expensive failures. Like the progress of aviation, it has its own tri-planes, *R101* airships and Bristol Brabazons, developments which in their time were hailed as prototypes for the future, but which in the event ended on the scrap heap or in history's locker room. Such were 'the draw', 'the leg volley' and 'the dog-stroke' and others that have succumbed to the test of long-term feasibility.

The dog-stroke, for instance, could be as hazardous as taking on a Messerschmitt with a Gloucester Gladiator, at least figuratively speaking. It involved cocking the left leg to a rising ball on the leg stump and clipping it under the raised limb behind the wicket where, at that period, there was unlikely to be a man on patrol. In his autobiography, G.L. Jessop claimed that the stroke was patented by an amateur batsman named C.O.H. Sewell, but in fact it had been employed earlier, notably by Richard Daft and Lord Harris. The latter admitted: 'It was a very dangerous shot, though I don't remember being hurt myself.' The risks in playing the stroke, before the box became accepted protective gear, can be readily imagined, but who actually invented the stroke need not concern us since it hardly survived the First World War. The last man recorded as playing it, and one can well believe it, was Learie Constantine against Lancashire in 1939, and he received a reprimand from his captain, R.S. Grant.

INTO THE DRIVE WITH FULLER PILCH

Let us move on to the men who created the strokes that have endured to this day. The drive is as good as any stroke with which to start. Unfortunately, early cricket writing is cloudy in its description of individual stroke-play, or at least it uses terms which do not always translate into modern idiom. The originator therefore has to be traced through a process of elimination.

We know that the great Alfred Mynn was not adept at the drive, off or cover, as it is understood today (i.e. moving, or taking two steps, out to the ball with the left leg leading). For it is reliably reported that while the Kent giant would leap threateningly into the air, he almost invariably landed back in the same place.

William Lambert of Surrey (1779–1851), notorious for allegedly 'selling' the England *v* Nottinghamshire match, was renowned for the power of his hitting. His readiness to attack the bowling puts him in line for recognition as a pioneer of the drive, except for one tell-tale piece of contemporary evidence which notes that while Lambert would advance his left leg far down the wicket, as if in preparation for a mighty drive, he would immediately pull it back into the crease. This embryonic off-drive was actually a piece of gamesmanship. 'He thought it put the

Fuller Pilch – a static portrait of a pioneer of powerful driving.

Alfred Mynn – a cricketing giant
who was chained to the crease.

bowler off his pitch,' wrote the Right Reverend H.H. Montgomery, yet
another divine upon whom we depend for enlightenment in this period.

By deduction we can narrow down the search for the father of the
drive to a Canterbury innkeeper by the name of Fuller Pilch, he of the
wide-open stance with which a much reproduced lithograph has made
us familiar. We have seen in an earlier section how William Fennex
countered David Harris' high bounce by going down the wicket to hit.
In this old pro's later years he would proudly claim that Fuller Pilch
was the inheritor of his forward style. 'I suspect,' writes the Reverend
James Pycroft, 'that Fuller Pilch may think he rather coincided with,
than learned from him.' In other words, there is the implication that
Fuller Pilch advanced things a great deal further than the Buckingham-
shire pioneer. We get some confirmation of this premise from Fred
Gale, another contemporary witness. 'I hardly ever saw him let off an
off-ball which was wide of the wicket, and he had a terrific hit between
middle-off and cover, which gained him many a four or five runs.'

Nothing is certain in early cricketing history, yet my money is on
Fuller Pilch as the man who discovered the rewarding boundary

between cover and mid-off (except that in his day there was no boundary). I admit that it would probably be a mistake to see him as a text-book example of the off- and on-drive as it is played today. Wickets in this period were notoriously unreliable. Pilch himself had to scythe and mow a meadow allotted for an All-England match in Glasgow, and was to be present at a Truro fixture where an outfielder put up a brace of partridges in the long grass. Then it could be argued that to be skilled enough to go driving in such conditions was an achievement in itself.

FELIX AND THE CUT

Fuller Pilch's partner in many a famous stand for the All England XI was Nicholas Wanostrocht. The scorers of the time found it more convenient to call him 'Felix', and this is the alias he used for his classic manual on the art of cricket, *Felix on the Bat*.

Here is Fuller Pilch writing admiringly of a batsman he was often privileged to be able to observe at first hand.

> It was a beautiful thing to see him [Felix] throw his right foot forward – for as you remember he was left-handed – and do a little tip-toeing with the bat over his shoulder, and if he did get the ball full you heard her hit the off-side palings as soon as she left the bat.

It seems to me, and many other better informed commentators, that what Fuller Pilch is describing here is the cut off the front foot. The deceptive speed with which the ball is reported to leave the bat is, of course, the major reward for the executor of the wristiest of strokes.

Writing about the cut, Felix quoted from *Macbeth*: 'If it were done when 'tis done, then 'twere well it were done quickly.' It would seem that he practised what he preached, off the front foot and on the back. The distinguished player and chronicler the Hon. R.H. Lyttleton had no hesitation in aclaiming Felix as 'the father of the cut', which should be authority enough for us. This is one innovator who has been easily traced.

All the same it may be worth looking closer into the ancestry of Felix's renowned wristwork. Analogies with fencing are a recurrent theme in *Felix on the Bat*. Indeed the author recommends a fencing posture as the ideal stance to adopt at the wicket. 'Observe the first position in fencing, "*En garde!*"'. How beautifully every limb of the body is prepared for action!' Felix goes on to urge his readers to attack the ball as one might a man in a metal mask – '*En garde!*', 'Lunge!', '*En garde!*'.

This Blackheath schoolmaster was a master of many skills – an artist, musician and engineer (he designed the first bowling machine). Can we doubt that he was also a handy man with the foil? So perhaps cricket owes a debt of gratitude to fencing, as well as to Felix. Together, it would seem, they introduced a necessary measure of swashbuckle to a game that had hitherto been mostly bludgeon.

THE LEG-SIDE PIONEERS

The honours for inventiveness in leg-hitting go to George Parr, captain of the All England XI and stalwart of Nottinghamshire where, at the old Trent Bridge ground, the shots he planted in this area were marked by a tree bearing his name. However, as the control of cricket moved from the professional impresarios to the gentlemen of Marylebone, batsmen were encouraged to resist the lure of the leg. Increasingly, the emphasis was placed on elegant off-side play. Hefty cross-batted swings tended to be greeted with 'tut, tuts' rather than with applause. Perhaps the new Establishment's subconscious desire was to sever cricket from its agricultural roots; thus, any stroke savouring of the cow-shot was suspect.

George Parr of Nottinghamshire and the All England XI. A tree was named after him at Trent Bridge.

Nº1. Series of Cricketers.

N F E L I X E S QRE

BORN AT CAMBERWELL IN SURREY

Felix with bat – he brought the wristwork of fencing to cricket.

At Eton in the 1890s, B.J.T. Bosanquet was severely reprimanded for pulling a ball on his off stump to leg. 'Boy, if you play like that I won't have you in the Eleven!' his cricket master warned. And as late as the mid 1920s, the young Walter Hammond, who had just hit up 250 mostly with leg shots, was told by informed authorities that he would never be selected for England unless he mended his ways.

It is this attitude which explains why, for so much of the Victorian era, bowlers tended to confine their attack on, or outside, the off stump. This was 'off theory', involving a packed off-side field with the leg side left almost unguarded.

THE SCANDALOUS E.M. GRACE

W.G. Grace was not a man to be overawed by convention, and it would be no surprise to learn that he was the first to upset this particular applecart. In fact, however, it was his older brother, E.M. Grace. To quote from *A History of Cricket* by H.S. Altham and E.W. Swanton:

Opposite: E.M. Grace and younger brother, a late convert to leg-hitting.

'From an early age he had shown himself impatient of the canons of orthodoxy in batting, and at the beginning of his career the critics were scandalized by his cross-hitting.'

The 'Coroner', as this Doctor Grace was known, had a highly effective method of dealing with 'off theory'. He would cart the ball to leg where, usually, there was only a token force in the field. Even the good-length ball on the off stump found itself streaking like a number two iron shot to the mid-on area. When the opposing captain finally decided to reinforce the unfashionable side, E.M. would demonstrate that he could drive through the covers as powerfully as any man.

The 'Coroner' pioneered territory that others would later find it fruitful to plunder; ultimately, these would include his brother, W.G. We know that W.G. could play the pull shot, because he says so in his book *Cricketing Reminiscences*; but he does so in a strangely apologetic manner, and there is more than a suggestion that the stroke is definitely for 'adults only', and pretty senior adults at that.

> Young batsmen should be severely reprimanded if they show any tendency towards pulling. Some of my readers may say; 'But I have seen W.G. himself pulling balls to leg.' My answer is that I have never pulled a ball until I was forty years of age.

Nothing, to my mind, better illustrates the strength of contemporary opposition to the cross bat than these few words of Grace's. The pull shot in these Victorian times was comparable to the brandy decanter on the sideboard, emphatically not for consumption by the sons of the house, though father might be excused a tipple after a tiring day. Elsewhere in his *Reminiscences* Grace mentions Mr W.W. Read among current batsmen who encouraged him to imbibe of this heady stroke – in moderation, of course – and here, I believe, the doctor has identified the man who made the pull shot almost respectable.

WALTER READ STRIKES

A BOLD BLOW FOR LEG HITTING

Perhaps if the Surrey amateur Walter Read had been allowed to go in a little earlier for England against Australia in the Oval Test of 1884 he would have played a more conventional innings, for he was an orthodox driver of the first calibre. However, for reasons which have never been properly explained, this splendid batsman was pencilled in at number ten.

Walter Read of Surrey and England. He proved that leg hits could save Test matches.

England were facing a hitherto unprecedented Australian total of 551 in this Oval game, and far from confidently. When Walter Read bustled impatiently to the crease, 8 wickets were down for 181. England were still 370 runs adrift. Whatever the causes of his demotion, all observers are agreed that Read's fury with his captain, Lord Harris, was transferred to the Australian bowlers, the rampant trio – at least up until now – of Palmer, Spofforth and Midwinter. For the benefit of the English authorities, and to the dismay of the Australian enemy, Read mounted a dazzling display of batting 'in the round'.

'It seemed to me,' he was to recall in later years, 'that with all the men on the off-side it was a thousand pities to neglect any opportunity of getting the ball to the on.' And this is exactly what Read proceeded to do. Enthused one reporter: 'His leg hitting, it may be said without exaggeration, was the most brilliant both for timing and power that has been seen since the days of George Parr.'

In little more than an hour, this tempestuous number ten overhauled the England opener, Scotton, who had managed 53 when the Surrey man arrived at the crease. An hour later Read had 117 on the board,

Scotton having advanced to 90. The match was saved and the Ashes were secured for England.

We read that in the later stages of this tremendous knock, enthusiastic members of the crowd were mingling with the hard-pressed Australian fielders and were persuaded to return to their seats only by Lord Harris' threat that 'if they did not get back he would give the game to Australia'. In the patriotic fervour of the moment, even the establishment die-hards seem to have overlooked the fact that Read had scored over half his runs on the 'wrong' side of the wicket. Later, old prejudices would return; but meanwhile, Walter Read had made the telling point that leg hits could save Test matches.

The men who change cricket tend to be imaginative thinkers as well as skilled players. Certainly, we know that Walter Read thought deeply about his craft. In order to liberate his batting from the constraints of off theory, he adopted the unusual method of imagining that the stumps did not exist. In this way he learned to play the conventional ball outside the off stump as if it were outside the leg and, consequently, ripe for pulling.

JACK HOBBS – THE QUIET REVOLUTION

Now for one of the most discreet revolutionaries in the history of the game – Sir Jack Hobbs. There are many photographs that illustrate the changes he brought about in accepted batting practice, but his essential technique is summarized in his stance. For comparative purposes, let us look first at the classic, 'golden age' stance of a batsman such as L.C.H. Palairet of Somerset.

Palairet was an amateur and, true to the amateur spirit, he was on the look-out for the drivable ball to the off. Thus, his shoulder is facing the bowler in a handsome posture which, however, has the drawback of limiting his field of vision to off-side territory. A fast rising ball on the leg stump could seriously discomfort this stylish player.

Now look at Hobbs' stance. Hobbs was a professional, and was looking for runs wherever he could find them. Runs were his business, after all. Thus, the shoulder has come round to face mid-on and both eyes are on the bowler with obvious advantages to the batsman's field of vision. It is an ideal stance for the complete batsman. Yet, believe it or not, it was regarded with some misgivings by the off-side brigade, who suspected Hobbs of being a 'two-eyed Jack', that is, a man with half his optical faculties on the unfavoured leg-side boundary.

Fortunately Hobbs carried a magic commendation around with him. 'He bats like an amateur,' Sir Pelham Warner had declared with the full weight of his authority. Thus Hobbs, who had more than proved himself on the off, was issued with a visa to explore the leg side without interference from the purists. As we can see, he was superbly positioned to do just that. When in the 1920s the conventional attack switched from off to 'leg theory' (a non-intimidatory version of Bodyline), Hobbs was the batsman who was best equipped 'to place this rubbish in the dustbin', as A.C. MacLaren put it.

THE HOOKER BECOMES A HERO

There is a strong case for arguing that it was the Bodyline version of leg theory which finally established the respectability of the pull and the hook. Less hampered by old school ties, the Australians had been developing the two shots for years on their faster, truer wickets. Now came the ultimate test of their capability. By its very nature – short, fast, directed on or outside the leg stump – Bodyline practically eliminated the option of conventional off-side play. So it was the cross bat that Stan McCabe chiefly employed in his legendary innings of 187 not out

The young J.B. Hobbs, alert to opportunities on the leg.

L.C.H. Palairet's orthodox stance.

Ranji's statue at Jamnagar, India.

against the full fury of Larwood and Voce in the First Test at Sydney in 1932. By all accounts, this was the most courageous and devastating response to intimidatory pace hitherto witnessed, and the perpendicular swing had played little part in it. In the circumstances, could anyone dare to raise an eyebrow at young Stan McCabe for pulling and hooking the most questionable form of attack England had ever mounted?

THE PRINCE OF GLANCERS

The stroke inventors, as we have seen, are not always easy to pinpoint with absolute confidence. Fennex and Pilch vie for the authorship of the off-drive, for instance, just as Thomas Edison and Louis Lumière contest the invention of the cinema. However, when it comes to the invention of the leg-glance, the finger points unhesitatingly to one man. His name is Prince K.S. Ranjitsinhji of Sussex and England. 'Not many people realise that Ranji left a greater impact on the game than anyone else,' wrote his gifted nephew, K.S. Duleepsinhji. This is possibly overstating the case, for understandable reasons of family pride and affection; yet there is no doubt that Ranji brilliantly remedied a serious deficiency in contemporary stroke-play.

No problems about the drive, as we have seen. Off theory nourished it, even if occasionally it caught it out. The cut was a going concern, though Ranji would certainly enhance it, and the swing to leg, again as we have seen, was already making good progress, even if it still had a long way to go for enthusiastic recognition from the Establishment. There remained the nagging problem of how to score from the good-length ball on the leg stump, assuming a desire to score.

The answer in the old days seems to have been the 'draw', already mentioned as one of batting's museum strokes. But this, which involved using the ball's own energy for generating runs, was never an easy stroke to play. Indeed, Felix's directions on how to execute it read like an elaborate recipe for a French dessert – 'as your body recedes, turn the face of the bat inwards, so as to describe an angle of 45 degrees with the parallelism of the wicket etc., etc.'. Well before the age of Ranji, the stroke had fallen out of use. For those who did not relish the perils of the dog-stroke, there remained, as W.G. Grace admits, the half-cock stroke, 'a purely defensive stroke, though runs are occasionally scored from it.'

Where Felix had turned to fencing for his inspiration, Ranji turned to the far unlikelier game of chess for the solution to passivity outside the leg stump. 'When your opponent attacks,' he noted, 'your aim should always be that your own move be not only defensive, but should have an attacking force of its own.'

Of course, Ranji had advantages other than a mere familiarity with chess. He had an eagle eye and extraordinarily flexible wrists. It was a combination of these two natural assets which could send a ball which might normally have been 'half-cocked' to silly mid-on, racing to the long-leg boundary – the leg-glance, in other words.

Ranji had another natural asset, and in his friend C.B. Fry's view, it was the crucial one – footwork. Ranji's glance off the front foot was an aggressive stroke in the fullest sense of the word. As he prepared to strike, the left leg sprang down the wicket to form a pivot on which the whole body, from the hip upwards, twisted to whip the ball behind the wicket for multiple runs.

This Prince of England batsmen was also the master, indeed the inventor, of the leg-glance off the back foot, a more familiar stroke to modern eyes. But if C.B. Fry is to be believed, no one could, or did, succeed in emulating him in either the front-foot or the back-foot stroke.

Opposite: K.S. Ranjitsinhji at the crease. The inventor of the leg-glance, but dominant all round the wicket.

RANJITSINHJI: BATTING STATISTICS

Century on debut for the county
1895	150	Sussex *v* MCC (Lord's)

Century in the first match of a tour
1897/8	189	A.E. Stoddart's XI *v* South Australia (Adelaide)

Century on debut in Test cricket
1896	154*	England *v* Australia (Manchester)

Century in each innings
1896	100 and 125*	Susses *v* Yorkshire (Hove) (on the same day – 22 August)

Three centuries in successive innings
1896	165	Sussex *v* Lancashire (Hove)
	100	Sussex *v* Yorkshire (Hove)
	125*	
1900	127	Sussex *v* Gloucestershire (Hove)
	222	Sussex *v* Somerset (Hove)
	215*	Sussex *v* Cambridge University (Cambridge)

Ten or more centuries in a season
1900	11 centuries
1896	10 centuries

Five double-centuries in a season
1900	275	Sussex *v* Leicestershire (Leicester)
	222	Sussex *v* Somerset (Hove)
	220	Sussex *v* Kent (Hove)
	215*	Sussex *v* Cambridge University (Cambridge)
	202	Sussex *v* Middlesex (Hove)

Double-century in successive innings
1900	222	Sussex *v* Somerset (Hove)
	215*	Sussex *v* Cambridge University (Cambridge)
1901	285*	Sussex *v* Somerset (Taunton)
	204	Sussex *v* Lancashire (Hove)

Thousand runs in Australia
1897	1157 runs (average 60.89)

Thousand runs in a month
1899	1037 runs (average 79.76) June
1899	1011 runs (average 77.76) August
1900	1059 runs (average 96.27) July

Three thousand runs in a season
1899	3159 runs (average 63.18)
1900	3065 runs (average 87.57)

Partnerships over two hundred
1902	344 with W. Newham	7th wkt *v* Essex (Layton)
1899	325 with G. Brann	2nd wkt *v* Surrey (Oval)
1901	298 with E. Killick	3rd wkt *v* Lancashire (Hove)
1901	292* with C.B. Fry	2nd wkt *v* Somerset (Taunton)
1904	255 with C.B. Fry	3rd wkt *v* Yorkshire (Sheffield)
1899	252 with G. Brann	2nd wkt *v* Gloucestershire (Bristol)

All partnerships were for Sussex.
Partnership of 344 with W. Newham is an England record for the seventh wicket.

Ranji's beautiful stroke-play and attacking game made him one of the hardest batsmen to dislodge, as the above statistics bear emphatic witness.

Source: *Ranji*, by Alan Ross, Collins, 1983.

Ranji was to enjoy one more advantage in the playing of the leg-glance which was given to few of his imitators. According to Neville Cardus, no trap was set for him. Apparently, Ranji was so dominant all round the wicket that the wretched bowlers reckoned that feeding these strokes was the only possible way of getting him out, hopefully by an lbw decision.

THE IRISH AUTHOR OF THE REVERSE SWEEP

It would have been appropriate to close this section with a stroke formulated in our own times. The reverse sweep was nominated, as patented by Ian Botham, as forbidden by the England chairman of selectors P.B.H. May, and as nevertheless put into production by England captain Mike Gatting to his cost in the vital World Cup final

Ian Botham practising a stroke invented by Sir Timothy O'Brien – the reverse sweep.

In defiance of all the text books! The modern 'making-room' stroke.

against Australia in 1987. However, investigation showed that the stroke has distant Irish antecedents, fittingly perhaps, as that country has given the world the back-handed wit of Oscar Wilde and George Bernard Shaw.

The Irishman in question was the Middlesex and England player Sir Timothy O'Brien (a nice Irish paradox in itself) who scored an aggressive 92 against the Australians while still in his first year at Oxford. O'Brien was a genial and humorous man with a temper that could turn as fierce as his batting. One afternoon when Middlesex were playing Gloucestershire, this temper turned on the Grace brothers, E.M. and W.G., who, fielding at point and first slip respectively, were carrying on a boorish conversation which O'Brien, who was batting, decided had been calculated to upset his concentration. The Irishman suddenly reversed his grip on the bat and left-handedly swept the ball at the ample midriffs of the two talkative brothers. The stroke must have scored runs, for it did not have to wait for the arrival of Botham or Gatting to be imitated. So it could be argued that if the Grace brothers had been more restrained, and Sir Timothy O'Brien less quick-tempered, Gatting may never have ventured the stroke that perhaps cost England its first World Cup title.

THE 'MAKING-ROOM' INNOVATION

So much for our attempt to attribute the reverse sweep to the 1980s. But there is still one stroke that no other era can claim as its own – the inelegant 'making-room' stroke, employed to smack a ball on, or outside, the leg stump to the off. Dozens of contemporary cricketers contend for authorship of this stroke, Derek Randall, Graham Gooch, Mike Gatting, Tom, Dick and Harry being prominent amongst them. But the real author is an influence without a human face: it is the remorseless demands of one-day cricket, a source of much entertainment but, nevertheless, a brutal destroyer of batting style.

6
LEADERS OF CHANGE

Not all the changes that cricket has witnessed have taken place out on the field. From the beginning, the game's direction, and indeed its future, has depended on its patrons and organizers. Hambledon might never have been created if a number of wealthy aristocrats had not decided to attract the best talent to this out-of-the-way Hampshire community. The MCC itself was the brainchild of a number of gentlemen of leisure meeting regularly in a tavern which, incidentally, was far from the present site of Lord's.

Later, the spread of cricket was continued by professional impresarios such as William Clarke and John Wisden, organizers of the great travelling elevens which brought cricket to town like the circus and strolling players of another kind. Later still, the control of cricket returned to lordly patrons, embodied in our own century in the persons of Lord Harris of Kent and Lord Hawke of Yorkshire. No responsible review of the men who changed the game can ignore these impressive noblemen; they stand like two heraldic carvings at the gates of modern cricket.

MY LORDS HARRIS AND HAWKE

The fourth Lord Harris was born in 1851, the seventh Lord Hawke nine years later. Both men were to come to dominate cricket until their deaths in the 1930s. The two men could fairly be described as somewhat reactionary in temperament, at least from our angle of cricketing history. Lord Hawke will always be remembered for his fervent prayer, 'Pray God no professional may ever captain England!' Lord Harris detected 'reds under the bed' even in a development as seemingly politically unmotivated as the young Walter Hammond's decision to play for Gloucestershire rather than his native Kent. 'Bolshevism is rampant and seeks to abolish all laws and rules, and this year cricket has not escaped its attack,' he warned. Yet the two men's shared passion for cricket probably contributed more than any other combination to its spread, through time as well as over space.

From the day he stepped into the breach to lead a disintegrating party of amateurs to Australia in 1878 (it had finally to be reinforced with two professionals who had not discovered previous engagements), Lord Harris made it his business to ensure that tours between the two countries were organized on an efficient and regular basis. We will read later of his momentous anger with the Sydney crowd during this pioneering tour. On the other hand, we have had a glimpse in the previous section of his good sportsmanship. This is a recurrent theme in contemporary descriptions of Tests in which he participated. In fact, Lord Harris' sporting example could be seen as crucial in determining the good spirit in which Anglo-Australian Tests have – with one or two notable exceptions – been played.

Lord Harris' word 'was almost law', according to Pelham Warner, and it cannot be doubted that the former had his say in most of the good

Lord Harris. His word was 'almost law'.

69

and bad decisions that were taken in English cricket in the first thirty years of the century, from the brilliant idea of leap-frogging Warner himself to the captaincy of England in Australia in 1903 to the disastrous dropping of A.P.F. Chapman in 1930. However, he was cruelly caricatured in the Australian *Bodyline* TV series, although in reality he could have had little to do with Jardine's appointment since he died five months before it was made.

Lord Hawke, meanwhile, claims our attention as cricket's greatest missionary. Usually off his own bat and out of his own pocket, he undertook tours of New Zealand, the West Indies, South Africa, Canada, the United States and the Argentine, and although he may have failed to light a blazing torch for cricket in all these countries his achievements in the propagation of the game are far-reaching.

It is certain that Lord Hawke's 'wider still and wider' designs for cricket went hand in hand with imperialist dreams. 'The future of cricket and the Empire is inseparably connected,' he said. If the Empire turned out to be a lost cause, cricket certainly gained from Lord Hawke's championship. Besides, his view of cricket was essentially noble – he saw it as an unrivalled unifier. 'High and low, rich and poor are practically on an equality in cricket,' he insisted.

Lord Hawke's other outstanding contribution to the health of the game was on a more local level. In 1883, as a young Cambridge graduate, he assumed command in a Yorkshire dressing room where the atmosphere was comparable to that which, in more recent times, reputedly drove Bill Athey and others to seek asylum in othe counties. In a few seasons he had converted a bickering Yorkshire team into the most formidable force in county cricket. At the turn of the century it would win the County Championship three years in succession.

Martin Hawke sometimes made himself unpopular down south by withholding the services of Hirst and Rhodes from vital Tests for what he considered were even more important county fixtures. Yet, as has often been said (perhaps it was Lord Hawke himself who coined the phrase), 'a strong Yorkshire is a strong England'. And so it has proved, notably at The Oval in 1938 where Yorkshire batsmen contributed 612 out of England's record total of 903 for 7 declared. The ghost of Lord Hawke seems to demand that such times will come again.

The smile on the face of the conqueror. Warwick Armstrong warming up against Leicestershire in 1921.

WARWICK ARMSTRONG AND

THE BEGINNINGS OF TOTAL WAR

From two formidable and influential Englishmen, let us turn to one outsize Australian – Warwick Armstrong, the architect of eight consecutive Test victories against England in the two series that followed the First World War. If Armstrong was noteworthy merely for crushing England, we might leave him there. After all, there's no point in dwelling on our defeats! But Warwick Armstrong's impression on Test cricket has been of a more permanent kind. He was the first captain, but by no means the last, to go into battle with pace at both ends. Until the Armstrong era it was the norm to couple pace with 'slows', on the assumption that there was nothing like variety to upset a batsman's timing.

It so happened that Armstrong had two of the fastest bowlers hitherto unleashed against England, J.M. Gregory and E.A. McDonald. Of the former, Gilbert Jessop, by this time sadly on the sidelines, would write, 'It's no secret that Mr Gregory, by reason of the shortness of his length, is suspect of being indifferent to the safety of opposing batsmen.' If England's management hoped that this ferocious pair would be blunted by a strenuous county programme, they were to be disappointed. Armstrong bowled trundlers against the Derbys and the Leicester-

Lord Hawke. He nursed 'wider still and wider' ambitions for cricket.

shires and nursed his speed kings for the Tests, itself an innovation in touring captaincy. Armstrong also had the services of a teasing spinner in A.A. Mailey, but he was reserved for mopping-up operations. The top batsmen in England's order saw little but speed, and of this some of them saw not very much.

The 22-stone Armstrong's impact on Test warfare is comparable to that of Napoleon on the more conventional kind. Before the advent of the Corsican military genius, it was simply not done to use concentrated artillery to tear out the enemy's heart, but this is what Napoleon did at Austerlitz and it is effectively what Warwick Armstrong did in the English season of 1921. The devastation that this ruthless new strategy

The nearly invincibles. Warwick Armstrong's Australian team in England, 1921.

wrought in English ranks can be measured by the fact that the panicking selectors capped as many as thirty-two players for five Test matches. It was said that England honours were easier to come by than county colours in that traumatic season.

Armstrong's method of attack in 1921 set the pattern for future Test offensives. It was a pretext for Jardine's Bodyline assault and a precedent for Bradman's and Hutton's grim pace bombardments in 1948 in England and 1954/5 in Australia, both building on Armstrong's principle of speed first and spin some way behind. A generation later, as we shall see, Clive Lloyd was to take the principle to extremes upon which even these Bonapartes might have frowned.

Warwick was nearing the end of his career in 1921. A lithe and athletic all-rounder in Australia's golden age, he now, in county matches at least, tended to nod off in the outfield after a largely liquid lunch, perhaps comfortable in the knowledge that he had changed the face of Test cricket.

In one respect only could Warwick Armstrong be said to have failed. He believed strongly that Test matches should, as the term implied, be fought to a finish. In the 1921 series they were allotted only three days. As England battled towards an honourable draw during the Fifth Test at The Oval, Armstrong showed his contempt of time limitations by picking up an evening newspaper and reading it from cover to cover. The point he was trying to make was lost on the Oval crowd; they thought he was just being rude, and jeered him into retirement. But the Armstrong style of captaincy was not to lie down.

ENGLAND'S FIRST PROFESSIONAL CAPTAIN

– AN ENDURING EXPERIMENT

Len Hutton of Yorkshire was appointed to lead England (provisionally for the First Test only) in the summer of 1952. He thereby became the first professional to captain England, although, as we have noted, Hobbs once deputized for an ailing Arthur Carr. The appointment represented not so much a sudden crumbling of the class barriers as an instinct that it might be time to fall in with Australian practice and put the team's best player in command. There could be no doubts about Hutton's eligibility on this score.

The choice of Hutton was not seen as an irrevocable switch to professional leadership. In the wings, as *The Cricketer* observed, was a trio of future amateur leaders – Peter May, David Sheppard and Colin Cowdrey – all of whom would assume the mantle in due course.

Meanwhile, Hutton's first season of England leadership was an unqualified success. A weak Indian team with no appetite for Trueman's pace was bundled out of contention with three England victories to nil. However, the real test of England's first professional skipper was to come the following summer, with Australia.

England had not won a Test series against Australia since Jardine's controversial victories in 1932/3. Now, the nation's hopes were high England had finally discovered a truly fast bowler in the young Fred Trueman and had two talented young batsmen of post-war vintage in

Sir Leonard Hutton of Yorkshire and England.

Peter May and Tom Graveney. Besides, it was Coronation year and England's turn to excel.

Most of this confidence seems to have evaporated as the first day of the Nottingham Test dawned – in fact, it was drizzling. The selectors lost their nerve and fielded a safety-first eleven without Trueman or Statham and, therefore, heavily dependent on Alec Bedser. England might still have won the game, which was ultimately rained off, thanks to an inspired blitz of 7 for 47 by Bedser in Australia's second innings. However, Lindwall had already dynamited the England batting line-up with the exception, of course, of Hutton.

Then began the oft-repeated refrain that too much was being asked of England's first professional captain. Too heavy a responsibility rested on his shoulders as a batsman, it was said, for him to be charged with the added burden of captaincy. Much of this sort of comment was well intentioned, but behind some of the commiseration was an old-school attitude that longed for the return of the lost amateur leader.

Officialdom thereupon made an extraordinary move to satisfy this longing. The nostalgists were not actually given an amateur captain, for Hutton was retained; but it could be argued that they were given something even better – the Chairman of Selectors in person. This august official named himself – or was persuaded to do so by his colleagues – among the England twelve for the Second Test at Lord's: Mr F.R. Brown, the previous unpaid captain of England.

There can be little doubt that Freddie Brown had the best motives for deciding to throw himself into the fight. He was, after all, a useful leg-spinner and a pugnacious bat, if vulnerable to fast yorkers. However, the distinguished Australian correspondent Jack Fingleton described the decision as 'completely staggering'. He suggested that since Hutton was being appointed on a Test-by-Test basis, the playing of the chairman of selectors signalled a lack of confidence in Hutton's leadership that could only damage his morale. The Second Test at Lord's therefore became a severe examination for Len Hutton personally, and of the cause he represented. On the second day of the match he appeared to be flunking it hopelessly.

Australia's first innings urgently needed to be wrapped up. Alan Davidson, in particular, needed to be pocketed because his daredevil batting was swinging the game away from England. If catches can be said to win matches, England forfeited all hope of victory that morning by dropping five. In three cases, the England captain was the culprit. He dropped a slash from Hassett at second slip off Wardle. At fine leg this normally safe pair of hands juggled vainly with a ball at comfortable chest height. He moved to a position at cover, but the catches followed him. He got both hands to an uppish drive from the troublesome Davidson, but the ball spilled from his tense grasp. Sir Leonard Hutton had celebrated his thirty-seventh birthday that week, yet he now found himself in the position of a junior executive on whom the chairman has dropped in to see how he handles a meeting. Poor Len handled this part of the agenda wretchedly. He returned to the pavilion for repairs to minor damages sustained from the missed opportunity presented him by Hassett. The pavilion swallowed him in total silence. Freddie Brown took charge, a substantial and impressive figure gesticulating commands which were noticeably obeyed at the double. The Australian tail was wound up with officer-class efficiency.

What Hutton's feelings were as he walked out to bat with Don Kenyon can only be imagined; he is uncommunicative in his autobiographies about this crucial career crisis. He was facing an Australian total of 346 and about to face Lindwall and Miller. The former was already busy marking out his menacing run. All the same, one suspects the silence at his back must have seemed at least as threatening. In the pavilion Hutton's future was now being discussed in whispers.

Hutton's 145 was one of the greatest innings played against extreme pace.

74

Frank Worrell.

Hutton, with the buoyant assistance of Tom Graveney, was 83 not out at close of play. The next day he went on to complete one of the greatest innings ever played against extreme pace in conditions favouring the bowlers. This immaculate 145 did not win the match for England (in fact, the game was drawn thanks to an epic last-day stand by Willie Watson and Trevor Bailey); but what it did do was to ensure Hutton's retention in the captaincy long enough for him to engineer two Ashes wins against Australia. And it had an even more significant result, which was to see to it that henceforth ability rather than background became the ultimate test of a man's fitness to captain England.

TWO WEST INDIAN ARCHITECTS OF CHANGE

For some years now, the West Indies has been the supreme sporting power. Its influence on cricketing attitudes and methods throughout the playing world has, not surprisingly, been considerable. This loose amalgam of former colonies, now mostly independent states, has had many fine cricket captains, but two stand out as major influences, not only on the game in the Caribbean but on the cricket universe. The two men shared a genius with the bat and no mean ability with the ball; both were supreme in man management and at providing the inspiration that wins Test matches. However, when we come to assess their influence, the similarities begin to disappear. Sir Frank Worrell and Clive Lloyd have presented the world with two quite different images of West Indian cricket.

In 1960 Sir Frank Worrell achieved a 'first' similar to that established by his fellow knight, Sir Leonard Hutton. Before he led the West Indies 'down under' in that Australian summer, no black player had ever been the West Indian captain. The tradition he broke was perhaps even more unjustifiable than the amateur captain tradition in England. Although the West Indies had produced a few outstanding white players, notably Jeff Stollmeyer and Gerry Gomez, these were far outnumbered by black skills. By the mid 1950s it was noticeable that the West Indies current captain, John Goddard, would have been unlikely to claim a place on playing merit alone.

Worrell's impact on the West Indian team was immediately felt. Island jealousies and rivalries were no longer tolerated. A team of many factions was taught the supreme virtue of cohesion.

Worrell's reforms were not solely directed towards the West Indies. He had looked around the playing world and had noticed that the joy was going out of the game. Too many Tests were being played too slowly in a sour, acrimonious atmosphere. Umpiring decisions, accusations of unfairness and pavilion wrangles were tending to make larger headlines than the game itself. It could be said that Worrell was looking at an international cricket scene not all that far removed from today's.

As an immediate remedy, he insisted that his team play the game. West Indian batsmen became notable for hustling from the crease after Gary Sobers had been severely reprimanded for loitering when the umpire's finger was raised.

Next, with the lively co-operation of Sir Donald Bradman and the Australian captain Richie Benaud, Worrell engineered one of the brightest and most exciting Test series that has ever been played. It included, of course, the astonishing Test tie at Brisbane, but most of the

Pitch invasion after a nail-biting finish. Second Test, England *v* West Indies at Lord's, 1963.

Clive Lloyd.

other Tests also had the spectators on the edge of their seats. Moreover, the 1960/1 Test series was played with an immense amount of goodwill. After it was all over, the two captains drove in cavalcade through cheering crowds. Australia had witnessed some dreary cricket in recent series, much of it, sadly, provided by England. Now it had rediscovered its love of the game.

Another great series followed in England. The Second Test at Lord's almost rivalled Brisbane for a nail-biting finish. Frank Worrell seemed to have that effect on a game. Worrell himself contributed few major innings and bowled little, but it hardly seemed to matter. And no one suspected that this once marvellous stroker of the ball was ailing. Sir Frank Worrell, recently knighted to the satisfaction of the entire Commonwealth, died of leukaemia at the cruelly early age of forty-two.

The newspapers found a number of handy phrases to describe both Worrell's West Indians and the teams that his successor, Gary Sobers, led. They were dubbed 'sunshine', 'carnival' or 'calypso' cricketers to the point of repetitious cliché. One can well understand how a younger

West Indian cricketer like Clive Lloyd might have found such unsolicited public relations both irritating and patronizing. Certainly, when he assumed the West Indies captaincy in 1975, Lloyd seems to have made up his mind that nobody would use the term 'carnival' when his team came to tour – a carve-up was rather what tended to be on offer.

Nevertheless, Lloyd himself brought sunshine to many grounds, in particular to the often overcast stadium of Old Trafford, for he was the pride of Lancashire as well as the Caribbean. Anyone who watched him leisurely driving Bob Willis, at full speed, back over his head into the Nursery Stand in a Lancashire–Warwickshire Gillette Cup Final at Lord's could not question the huge entertainment value his batting brought to cricket. This batting might have led his admirers to anticipate a cavalier commander when he replaced Rohan Kanhai as West Indies' leader; in the event, he turned out to be more a Cromwell or a super Warwick Armstrong.

Worrell had two alarming fast bowlers in Wes Hall and Charlie Griffith of the javelin action, enough to make batting against the side a less than sunny experience. But Worrell also had the splendid off-spinner Lance Gibbs, and Gary Sobers who could bowl fast or slow, seam or spin – or just about anything that was asked of him. Variety was the spice of this West Indian attack.

Under Lloyd, non-stop speed was introduced with occasional 'guest' appearances by Roger Harper. It is possible to argue that Lloyd's

CLIVE LLOYD: CAREER STATISTICS

AS WEST INDIES CAPTAIN:

Year	Opponents	Matches	Won	Lost	Drawn
1974/5	India	5	3	2	0
1975	Pakistan	2	0	0	2
1975/6	Australia	6	1	5	0
1976	India	4	2	1	1
1976	England	5	3	0	2
1977	Pakistan	5	2	1	2
1978	Australia	2	2	0	0
1979/80	Australia	2	2	0	0
1980	New Zealand	3	0	1	2
1980	England	4	1	0	3
1980	Pakistan	4	1	0	3
1981	England	4	2	0	2
1981/2	Australia	3	1	1	1
1983	India	5	2	0	3
1983	India	6	3	0	3
1984	Australia	4	3	0	1
1984	England	5	5	0	0
1984/5	Australia	5	3	1	1
Total		74	36	12	26

AGAINST EACH COUNTRY:

	Played	Won	Lost	Drawn
Australia	22	12	7	3
England	18	11	0	7
India	20	10	3	7
New Zealand	3	0	1	2
Pakistan	11	3	1	7

Lloyd reigned supreme in the era of the West Indian fast bowlers. He has steered more Test sides to victory than any other captain in the history of the game.

Source: *Clive Lloyd – The Authorised Biography*, by Trevor McDonald, Granada, 1985.

Clive Lloyd wide awake in the field.

captaincy tenure coincided with a population explosion of West Indian fast bowlers. Andy Roberts was followed in quick succession, literally, by Michael Holding, Wayne Daniel, Colin Croft, Joel Garner and Malcolm Marshall. It could be argued that Lloyd's teams simply reflected the direction that Caribbean talent was taking. In other eras, however, these strike men would have had to wait their turn, as Tyson, Loader and Moss in the days of England's speed glut had to wait for Trueman and Statham to pull a ligament or retire. Under Lloyd's captaincy all stood a good chance of selection, because Lloyd defied the age-old insistence on a balanced attack. The policy certainly won matches; Clive Lloyd is undoubtedly the most victorious captain in Test history.

At the same time, his team did become one of the less magnetic attractions on the Test roster, at least when it was in the field. The over rates slowed. Even batsmen who had managed to get their eye in found it difficult to maintain momentum, and the crowds were starved of variety and those changes of tempo essential to the enjoyment of a cricket match.

Then came those incidents that full-throttle, overheated bowling is always liable to provoke: Holding's kicking over the wicket and the subsequent ructions in New Zealand, for example, and the blatant intimidation of Edrich and Close at Old Trafford in 1976. These were aberrations that Worrell would have moved swiftly to check. Lloyd, however, appeared to keep his own counsel.

It is possible that Clive Lloyd's influence on cricket will prove to be even more far-reaching than Frank Worrell's. Whether this will be for the better or the worse is for you, the jury, to decide.

IAN CHAPPELL AND

THE 'PLAYER POWER' REVOLUTION

Through all the fury of the West Indies on the attack, Clive Lloyd himself maintained a detached and courteous demeanour, which could not always be said of a contemporary Australian captain, Ian Chappell. Ian started out with the twin advantages of great talent and a useful family connection. He was the grandson of Victor Richardson, a former captain of Australia and a courageous rather than fluent bat who had had many proud bruises to show for his encounters with Larwood and Voce in the Bodyline series.

On his first tour of England in 1968, Ian Chappell came second only to his adhesive skipper, Bill Lawry, with 43.50 and an aggregate of 348 runs which had mostly been scored at moments crucial to Australia's retention of the Ashes. Even at this time he must have been viewed by the Australian authorities as the man best qualified in every respect to succeed Bill Lawry as captain. This, in due course, he was to do, though he did not turn out to be a captain in the style that had been anticipated.

Chappell led Australia for the first time in England in 1972. The tour was a great success, particularly in terms of goodwill and sportsmanlike behaviour. 'Ian Chappell,' *Wisden* reported, 'was a pleasing personality whose leadership on the field matured as the tour progressed.' The result, too, was pleasing for both sides: England 2, Australia 2.

The years between this summer and the Australian summer of 1974/5, when England returned the visit, seem to have effected a profound change in the captaincy and personality of Ian Chappell. Compare *Wisden*'s flattering comment with that below from H.L. Hendry, a member of Warwick Armstrong's team and now an Australian Test veteran of eighty summers.

Ian Chappell. 'He nudged cricket in the direction of gang warfare,' says Mike Brearley.

> As an ardent believer in the way cricket was meant to be played – and *was* played until disruptive tactics were introduced – I declare that I am utterly disgusted with the tactics adopted by Australia's present fast bowlers and captain.

Writing in *The Cricketer* in the aftermath of the savaging of Mike Denness' England tourists, Hendry continued:

> At the outset of the 1932 Tests our Board of Control screamed to the world in protest at Larwood and Voce's bowling. Yet not one word of condemnation has been uttered against our players today. One might be pardoned for thinking that the administrators have lost control and are afraid to discipline players; it is well known that the Australian captain has been reported to them on more than one occasion and has received no more than a few gentle words of warning.

Chappell was leading a team whose two strike bowlers had openly proclaimed they enjoyed hitting batsmen. Dennis Lillee revealed that

he aimed 'somewhere between the rib cage and the stomach', while Jeff Thomson confessed to a fondness for felling Englishmen. There is no record of a captain's reproof.

Even in appearance Chappell's team had undergone a transformation. Vanished were the clean-shaven men of 1972 – hair was now worn long, and walrus moustaches were in fashion. The team had a shaggy, raffish air that called to mind the patrons of the Ball and Bat on their once-a-year fixture issuing on to the ground from the public bar shortly after closing time. In action, of course, there was no such comparison. England were beaten four to one. Dennis Amiss was put out of the Second Test with a broken thumb and Lancashire's David Lloyd was virtually battered out of Test cricket.

Meanwhile, the Aussie fans were encouraged to applaud the achievements not of Australia but of 'Chappell's mob'. In other words, 'player power' had arrived. The selectors took a back seat, seeming to leave the direction of Australian cricket in the hands of a 'gang of four' – Chappell, Marsh, Lillee and Ian's brother Greg. Yet increasingly, Ian Chappell felt compelled to show his disregard for authority – once even with bared posterior. This was strange in a man who did, after all, occupy the enviable position of captain of Australia. At the height of his career, Ian Chappell seems to have discovered that he was a natural rebel. It was as if Robin Hood had suddenly taken to leading the Sheriff of Nottingham's men.

Ian Chappell batting in Packer colours.

Ian Chappell's style of leadership gained many victories. His team is the last to have competed on equal terms against the West Indies. Ultimately, however, there was a price to pay. The 'player power' revolution had been successful in placing extraordinary control in the hands of Chappell and his associates. Thus, when Kerry Packer approached the leader of the mob, he was able to acquire the Australian team lock, stock and barrel. And here began the long decline of Australian Test cricket.

MIKE BREARLEY AND THE

'BRAINS OVER BRAWN' REVIVAL

'In many ways he was an inspiring, tough and shrewd captain; but he also nudged cricket in the direction of gang warfare.' This is Mike Brearley writing about Ian Chappell in his book, *The Art of Captaincy*. Brearley himself can take credit for nudging cricket back into more tranquil pastures. He was also responsible for a heartening revival in England's Test fortunes. Some of his victories were achieved against Packer-weakened sides, but he twice masterminded the defeat of Australia at full strength.

The 1981 series against Kim Hughes' team was his golden summer as England's captain, as it was to be for Ian Botham and Bob Willis as players. The participants have provided many examples of his acumen: the calming advice to Chris Old to play his natural game in the chilling tension of the Headingley Test; and the handling of Botham, a reluctant dragon at Edgbaston ('the others are bowling better'), prior to a sensational 5 wickets for 1 run in 28 balls.

But perhaps the most telling illustration of his methods is the fact that in both these Tests, defending totals that left no margin for one long-hop, he bowled spinners – Willey at Headingley and Emburey at Edgbaston. The Middlesex off-spinner was to reward him with the crucial wickets of Border and Yallop. As Richie Benaud points out in an instructive chapter on captaincy (*Benaud on Reflection*, Willow Books), the safe alternative would have been to give the ball to Bob Willis or Chris Old and keep the game closed up. Brearley's victories were founded on the old-fashioned principle of the balanced attack.

It worried him that his contribution with the bat was modest in comparison with his leadership input. Indeed, it comes as something of a surprise to note that he joins Bradman and a mere twelve others in *Wisden*'s list of batsmen who have scored over 300 in a day – 312 not out for MCC Under-25 *v* North Zone at Peshawar in 1966. On the other hand, it could be argued that Brearley's moderate batting in the Tests where he captained helped to underline the fact, at a timely moment for cricket, that brainpower can rival brawn in the winning of Test matches. We have already discussed two captains contemporary with Brearley under whose leadership cricket seemed to be hurtling away from subtlety and imagination. Here, Captain Brearley provided a vital corrective.

KEITH CARMODY – THE 'UMBRELLA' MAN

Finally, we should salute an innovative captain who never led his country. His name was Keith Carmody of the 'Carmody umbrella' or 'field'.

The closest that Flight Lieutenant D.K. Carmody got to national cricketing leadership was as captain of the Royal Australian Air Force team in wartime Britain (he was Keith Miller's commanding officer) and as vice-captain to Lindsay Hassett in the 1945 'Victory' Tests. In fact, Carmody missed the first two of these, although he made strenuous

Mike Brearley, clearly in
command.

efforts to be present. Shot down off the Dutch coast in 1944, he was
finally freed by the advancing Russians from a POW camp where he had
made frequent escape attempts.

However, Carmody was to have the satisfaction of leading the once
poor relation of Aussie cricket, Western Australia, to capture the
Sheffield Shield trophy. The newcomers to the contest employed a
totally novel field setting, an arc of eight crouching fielders extending
from gully to leg gully waiting for snicks off the fast bowling. The
'Carmody umbrella' was soon adopted by Keith Miller, captain of New
South Wales, and before long became a feature of Australia's Test
attack.

Keith Carmody died in 1977. Ray Robinson, who wrote his obituary
in *The Cricketer*, accounted him the second Australian among cricket's
six great innovators, the first being J.McC. Blackham, the pioneer of
close-up wicket-keeping.

7
INQUEST ON PACKER AND 'WORLD SERIES CRICKET'

Counsel for the prosecution: Members of the jury, it is our intention to demonstrate to your complete satisfaction that Mr Kerry Packer's 'World Series' was responsible for causing grievous bodily harm to international cricket and, but for the intervention of circumstances, could have led to the tragic death of Test cricket itself.

Let me invite you to cast your minds back to the early summer of 1977 when the scale of the accused's machinations first became apparent. Three Australian journalists who were accompanying their national team in this country felt so strongly about events that they inserted the following notice in the London *Times*.

> In affectionate remembrance of International cricket which died at Hove, 9th May 1977. Deeply lamented by a large circle of friends. RIP.
> NB: The body will be cremated and the Ashes taken to Australia and scattered around the studio of TCN 9.

The men at the centre of the storm – Kerry Packer and his lieutenant, Tony Greig.

The allusion to Hove is a reference to Mr Tony Greig's press conference in that resort where the enormity of the accused's signings was revealed. These

84

Floodlit cricket – Kerry Packer's
lasting innovation.

included, as will be remembered, practically the entire Australian and West Indies teams and significant names from England, Pakistan and South Africa. 'TCN 9' is, of course, Mr Packer's Australian television station, Channel 9 – the failure of which to obtain a concession to cover Test matches in Australia induced the accused to make a deliberate attempt to wreck Test cricket itself.

Counsel for the defence: Objection, m'lud! My learned friend has no right to attribute these motives to my client. It was far from his intention to deprive the Test nations of the services of his players. On 9 May at Sydney Mr Packer clearly stated: 'These players will be available to play Test cricket, Sheffield Shield and club cricket when they are not required for the Super Tests.'

Counsel for the prosecution: That was hardly a practical suggestion, considering the extended programme envisaged by these so-called 'Super Tests'.

Counsel for the defence: Naturally my client looked for some give and take on the part of the official authorities. Mr Packer went out of his way to be conciliatory. He is on record as saying: 'We would like to fit in with the Board of Control and juggle playing dates.'

Counsel for the prosecution: Mr Packer juggled with more than playing dates!

Counsel for the defence: M'lud, I object!

Judge: Objection sustained. Learned counsel will be so good as to confine himself to the facts.

Counsel for the prosecution: The facts of the matter, m'lud, are that 51 of the world's leading players were swept, at a stroke, from the 'board' of Test cricket. I submit that this was not the act of a man who had the wider interests of cricket at heart. The accused is, on all the evidence, an extremely successful and shrewd businessman. He would have been well able to assess the financial damage he was inflicting on traditional cricket.

Counsel for the defence: My learned friend chooses to ignore the significant financial benefits my client introduced to what had hitherto been a notoriously underpaid profession. We hear of cricket's 'golden age'. I can assure the jury that there was little gold for the professional players who made it possible. Indeed, many were to die in penury and in some cases to take their own lives. I refer to the tragic deaths of Arthur Shrewsbury of Notts, John Briggs of Lancs and . . .

Counsel for the prosecution: Objection!

Judge: Learned counsel is quite right. This is irrelevant and inadmissible evidence.

Counsel for the defence: Then let me come to the nub of the matter. Before the advent of 'World Series Cricket', a player's fee for a Test-match appearance was £210. It was immediately increased to £1000, a move which Mr Tony Greig declared 'would have taken 100 years' in other circumstances. Before 'World Series Cricket', the maximum a player could expect to earn in an English season – exclusive of Test appearances – was in the region of £4000, though earnings of £2500 were not uncommon. This niggardly scale of remuneration was to be significantly improved, thanks to Mr Packer's championship of the players' cause. It is no secret that an average fee for a season with my client's 'World Series Cricket' was £18,000, a very substantial advance on what was on offer from official bodies.

Moreover, the Packer organization made no stipulation as to the number of days wives and families were permitted to accompany players on tour; whereas the TCCB imposed a limit of 21 days. I invite members of the jury to put themselves in the places of the men who said 'yes' to this new deal, and to ask themselves if, in all honesty, they would have decided otherwise.

(The defence now calls witnesses.)

Mr Alan Knott (a Packer recruit) stated that the demands of conventional Tests had almost led to the break-up of his marriage due to the enforced separations of touring.

Mr Derek Underwood (another 'World Series' contracted player) said that a cricketer approaching the end of his career was bound to consider his future: 'It's the biggest worry in my life, and I have no academic qualifications.'

New methods of marketing cricket – poster portraits of Tony Greig, Clive Lloyd and Ian Chappell promote 'World Series Cricket'.

Mr John Snow (a Packer recruit on the point of retirement from first-class cricket) stated that the only future open to him was umpiring, a prospect which he dreaded.

'Witness for the defence' Alan Knott catches Redpath off Clive Rice in the Grand Final 'Super Test', Sydney, February 1979.

Counsel for the prosecution: This is moving testimony, no doubt, and I should make it clear that the prosecution does not deny that 'World Series' players were generously rewarded. I merely ask you to consider the cost to orthodox cricket. I would like to draw the jury's attention to the rules formulated for 'World Series Cricket'.

Counsel for the defence: M'lud, I cannot see the point of this exercise. The rules were similar to those applied in other Test series.

Counsel for the prosecution: Except in one small but significant respect. They permitted the bowling of bumpers against *tailenders*!

From the outset we were given notice of the type of cricket that could be expected in the so-called 'Super Tests'. It was to be of the gladiatorial kind so much favoured by Mr Ian Chappell and his associates, a version of the game – I will not say a *perversion* – that rejoiced in confrontation and physical threat, that sought, in brief, to promote the less edifying features of modern cricket at the expense of its traditional virtues. Let me call a witness, Mr Michael Brearley, the former captain of England.

Mike Brearley: I have always believed that Packer offered some bold ideas to the cricket scene, both in content and in packaging. And he was successful in bringing a wider audience to the game. But in the process, 'World Series Cricket' set out to fuel the more elemental passions of the crowds. The television coverage, generally excellent as it was, still tended to linger lovingly on moments of violence and injury.*

Counsel for the defence: I have no questions, m'lud.

Counsel for the prosecution: Thank you, Mr Brearley. Let me turn now to another, and perhaps the most radical, defect in 'World Series Cricket' – that it

*From *The Art of Captaincy* (Hodder & Stoughton)

Tony Greig – reduced to England's ranks, but captain of the World XI.

Packer balcony scene. Mike Denness, manager of the World XI, talks tactics with his blue shirts.

was rootless. It helped itself to the pick of a year's crop and left the impoverished cricket authorities to nurture the future of the game as best they could.

Counsel for the defence: Once again, my learned friend is seeking to mislead the jury. From the beginning my client made it clear that the incentives he was offering would be widely spread. In particular, he offered a large investment in coaching schemes.

Counsel for the prosecution: There were many attractive items in Mr Packer's shop window. I am more concerned to identify the nature of the threat that lay behind the window dressing. Allow me to quote from my learned friend, Mr Michael Kempster QC, at the High Court hearing of October 1977: ' "World Series Cricket" is essentially parasitic in its nature. Its raw materials are and can only be the established players whose reputations and skills have been nurtured in playing conventional cricket games.'

Counsel for the defence: I am grateful to my learned friend for having drawn the jury's attention to this case, because it perfectly illustrates the rash and spiteful attitude adopted by the authorities at that time. It will be recalled that the TCCB, with the encouragement of the International Cricket Conference, made it their aim to ban the players who had enlisted with my client, not only from participating in Test cricket but from their livelihood in county cricket. It may also be recalled that, on appeal by the players, the High Court adjudged the authorities to be in serious contravention of existing employment legislation.

Counsel for the prosecution: It was certainly a desperate action, but I submit it was the accused who had made the authorities desperate. They believed – rightly, the jury may feel – that they were engaged in a life-and-death battle, the life and death of cricket. In the circumstances, can anyone censure the authorities for seeking to demonstrate to the deserters that they could not have their cake and eat it?

But let me come to the acid test of Mr Packer's dangerous experiment – its viability in the long term. I put it to you that 'World Series Cricket' lamentably failed this crucial test. As should have been obvious from the start, it lacked the

essential attraction of two fully representative teams pitted against one another in a genuine test of comparative skills. It offered instead a 'circus' of polyglot abilities. As soon as the accused got what he wanted in the first place, namely the concession to cover official Test matches, the whole expensive enterprise was abandoned, though we are, alas, still obliged to live with the so-called 'merchandising improvements' the accused has introduced to the game.

Counsel for the defence: M'lud, it is the defence's submission that 'World Series Cricket' resulted in nothing but good. It brought the game to a new public. At the same time, it obliged the existing authorities to adopt a more businesslike attitude and seek adequate sponsorship from companies like the Prudential. Today, cricketers throughout the world enjoy substantially improved rewards for the dedication they give to the game – thanks to my client!

The jury is still out. It is still perhaps too early for a final verdict on Packer, though there can be little doubt that he has influenced modern cricket more than any full-time administrator. Whatever its longer-term effects, it has to be admitted that 'World Series Cricket' in its 'Super Test' form was not a conspicuous success. Its failure to inspire the enthusiasm of genuine cricket lovers probably stemmed from the inability to sign the complete England cricket team, despite the best efforts of Packer himself and his recruiting sergeant, Tony Greig.

This shortcoming became more apparent when, contrary to expectations, England under Brearley's leadership convincingly defeated Australia three to nil in the 1977 series – all the more upsetting from a Packer viewpoint since, with two exceptions, the entire Australian team was earmarked for 'World Series Cricket'. When negotiations had started at the Melbourne Centenary Match in March of that year it had been assumed that Australia was the superior team in the context of the Ashes. Now, in order to get the public pulse racing, Kerry Packer really needed to be able to lay on a genuine opportunity for the 'Chappell mob' to avenge the defeat in England.

Some significant England players were, indeed, recruited. The valuable Kent contingent, Woolmer and Underwood were enlisted to a

Another item in Packer's 'shop window' – a mobile refreshments trolley.

Above and below: Packer cricket. Piracy? Or a better deal all round?

man. They were later joined by Warwickshire's Dennis Amiss and John Snow of Sussex, no longer a member of the England Test squad. Of course, Packer also had Tony Greig, the deposed England skipper who, even though reduced to the ranks, was still a useful member of the winning combination.

Boycott, Willis, Botham, Randall and the victorious captain, Brear-

ley, would have completed a grand sweep. In fact, we learn that direct approaches were made to Brearley during the Headingley Test with the aim of bringing the whole team into the Packer camp. But Mike Brearley declined to act as another Tony Greig (captain and under-cover recruiter); Geoffrey Boycott, who had recently decided to return to the England side, took a strong patriotic line. Bob Willis wavered, but was steadied by a whip-round of the hat at Edgbaston. It was not certain whether either Botham or Randall was even approached.

Be this as it may, England was able to send a strong and reasonably representative side to play 'official' Tests against Australia in 1978/9. It competed against a home team which had been effectively stripped of stars. Nevertheless, this team of no-hopers snatched a thrilling victory in the Third Melbourne Test, thanks to a century from Wood and the hostile bowling of Hogg and Dymock. I believe it was at this point that the paint began to peel from the Packer bandwagon. Australian hearts were bound to swell a little at this conventional Test cricket victory, and Australian heads were bound to ponder circumstances that prevented the Chappells, Lillee, Thomson and Walters from riding to the support of Graham Yallop and his gallant but hard-pressed band.

Meanwhile, 'World Series Cricket', though able to field complete Australian and West Indies teams, did not have a side representing England. A compromise 'World XI', over-stuffed with Packer's haphazard global signings, became the third competitor. The team was admittedly captained by a former England skipper, Tony Greig, but his lack of personal success in the series was tragic, considering his commitment to this new form of cricket.

It is tempting to suggest that Packer's 'Super Tests' finally foundered on the forward defensive prod of Geoffrey Boycott and also that of his captain, Mike Brearley.

Empty seats at a Packer 'Super Test'. Would a representative England team have filled these stands?

Opposite: The Gatting/Rana
confrontation, Faisalabad,
December 1987.

Test matches have often been marred by umpiring controversy, but up until 9 December 1987 at Faisalabad, Pakistan, none has been brought even to a day-long standstill. It may be that the events of this dire Test match will lead, eventually, to lasting improvements in the player–umpire relationship. On the other hand, it could represent a further milestone, perhaps the most significant so far, on a downhill path. What is certain is that umpire Shakoor Rana has already made a profound impact on modern cricket.

From the very beginning it was recognized that an umpire's lot is not an easy one. As William Clarke, the manager of the first All-England XI, was to remind the would-be adjudicator: 'There are some (and they ought to know better) who never are out unless the bowler makes the middle stump a summerset.' As recently as the previous section, we have seen how the prospect of donning the white coat drove the England fast bowler John Snow into the arms of Kerry Packer's 'World Series Cricket'.

Umpiring disputes – and by this we mean demonstrations that go far beyond the traditional shaking of the head as the wronged lbw victim returns to the pavilion – are by no means confined to the twentieth century. We read of extraordinary, yet oddly familiar happenings in 1878 during an Australian visit to Philadelphia, USA. As the climax to mounting frustration with the American adjudicators, the Australians staged a walk-off that turned into full-scale industrial action. Strong pressure, including threats of legal action, from the US authorities finally persuaded the Australians back on to the field but, as at Faisalabad, too late to produce a result. The Australians departed to the accompaniment of jeers from this pioneering fixture.

These globe-trotting Aussies belonged to the same party that had inflicted a surprise defeat on the MCC at Lord's in May of that year, in a match we shall be recalling shortly. During this England tour there had been similar complaints about umpiring standards. It was alleged that as professionals all English umpires were, by the nature of their employment, in the pockets of the amateur managers of the game.

This may have been overstating the case, yet we get curious confirmation of this uneasy relationship in the early career of the great English umpire Frank Chester (1896–1957). Some fifty years after this Australian tour, Chester was standing in his first county match, Essex *v* Somerset at Leyton. During the course of the game he had occasion to give both captains out – J.W.H.T. Douglas of Essex lbw and J. Daniell of Somerset stumped. 'Young man, you'll be signing your death warrant if you go on like that!' Chester's senior colleague at the other end cautioned.

THE INFLUENCE OF FRANK CHESTER

Frank Chester, a fine pre-First World War all-rounder for Worcestershire, is regarded as a major influence on the improvements brought

The close involvement of umpire Frank Chester. G.O. Allen is the bowler.

about in umpiring standards during this century. There would seem to have been plenty of room for improvement, leaving aside the implications of the anecdote just reported. The 1890s witnessed a pitch invasion at Lord's when the Middlesex amateur C.P. Foley was given out, 'handled the ball', by umpire Edward Henty, though in fact, he had played it with the middle of the bat. The most revealing feature of this incident was the reaction of the opposing Sussex skipper, W.L. Murdoch, who back in the pavilion suggested, 'Would you like to go in again, Cyril?' The umpire's word was apparently still not law.

There was also a strong element of pathos to the distinguished umpiring career of Frank Chester. Tipped as a future England player, he lost his right arm below the elbow in action in the First World War. Often as he crouched low over the wicket, the better to follow the flight of the ball, he must have wished it was he himself making the delivery, for he had captured 44 wickets cheaply in his first season for Worcestershire as well as scoring three centuries at the age of only seventeen.

Umpires have provided some of the game's best wisecracks. 'The only person who appeals more than you is Doctor Barnado,' remarked umpire Bill West to Yorkshire's Emmott Robinson. To Chester is attributed the famous witticism at the expense of Hedley Verity when, under a hammering from South Africa's H.B. Cameron, he was told: 'You had him in two minds there, Hedley – he didn't know whether to hit you for four or six!'

But cricket was not all light-hearted for Frank Chester. Towards the end of his career he developed stomach ulcers and was often officiating in some pain. Perhaps this was the root cause of his irritability with the Australian tourists in 1953; he disliked their demonstrative style of appealing and didn't trouble to hide the fact. Here we draw closer to Faisalabad territory. The Australians took exception to what they regarded as Chester's hostile attitude during the closely contested Fourth Test at Leeds and formally requested that he should not officiate at the Fifth Test at The Oval. As with a similar request from Pakistan in the summer of 1987, this was refused. Umpire Chester's name was duly announced as one of the two umpires for the Ashes decider at The Oval. However, the Australian captain Lindsay Hassett, usually the most affable of men, stuck grimly to his guns. Chester was persuaded to be diplomatically indisposed.

Walter Hammond. His request for a change of umpires was 'churlishly' refused.

THE OBJECTION TREND

Objection and counter-objection to umpires is an important strand in the sequence of events that leads to Faisalabad. In the Anglo-Australian context it started seven years before the Chester incident, at Brisbane in 1946 when umpire Eric Borwick turned down a convincing appeal against Bradman, then struggling on 28 in his comeback to Test cricket. The Australian Board of Control, 'churlishly' in Jack Fingleton's view, refused Walter Hammond's request that umpire Borwick should not officiate in the remaining Tests.

So with two little words from umpire Borwick ('not out'), a process of tit for tat began. And thus it has also been in the not always happy history of England v Pakistan Tests. We know that Pakistan have objected to the appointment of one or two English umpires, and it is certain that England in Pakistan have done the same.

A 1956 tour did not get off to the best of starts when on the night of 26 February at Peshawar a bucket of water was emptied over umpire Idris Begh, the first time anything of the kind had been perpetrated. The culprits were a party of MCC 'A' Team tourists led by Donald Carr, more recently a TCCB official. There is abundant evidence that Donald Carr and his pranksters considered themselves more sinned against than sinning. All the same . . .

This potentially explosive incident was successfully defused, perhaps because it was handled by two distinguished military commanders, Field Marshal Lord Alexander of Tunis in his role of President of the MCC and General Iskander Mirza of the Pakistan Board of Control. Nevertheless, the drenching of Begh entered, unhelpfully, into local folklore.

THE SPREAD OF DISSENT

Of course, a number of roads lead to Faisalabad and, with perverse geography, one route seems to take a long detour through New Zealand. Feathers flew at Dunedin and Wellington when Ian Chappell's Australians toured Kiwi-land. But these dust-ups were mild in comparison with the traumatic tantrums of the West Indies *v* New Zealand Test at Christchurch in 1980. It featured such unedifying spectacles as the demolition of a wicket by the toecap of Michael Holding ('no other cricketer could manage to make such a deplorable action look so graceful' observes Mike Brearley in his caption to the picture of the kick), a players' lock-in, and last, but by no means least in offensiveness, the butting of an umpire by fast bowler Colin Croft. It can be seen that events are tracing an escalation in disrespect for white-coated authority.

Soon a campaign began, which was to become clamorous after Faisalabad, for neutral umpires, or officiators representing both sides. Curiously enough, however, one of the first and fiercest umpiring incidents took place when an English umpire was standing in Australia. The year was 1879. Indeed, the riot that umpire Coulthard's raised finger provoked on the Sydney cricket ground may have persuaded the administrators to abandon the experiment of including a home umpire

Feathers fly at Dunedin. The footwork is by Michael Holding.

on an away tour, though the practice is still sedulously observed in school and village cricket circles.

HASIB AHSAN'S ROAD TO FAISALABAD

It's time to return to the road to Faisalabad and fall into step with a fellow traveller who has a pressing appointment with Mike Gatting and his sorry men. His name is Hasib Ahsan, and he is destined to star as the Pakistan team manager in the Faisalabad horror show. But we first encounter him as a young off-break bowler in Javed Burki's Pakistan team in England in 1962. Here again we touch upon vexed umpiring matters. Hasib Ahsan's name appears on the scorecard of the MCC *v* Pakistan match at Lord's, 19–22 May, where he is recorded as taking 0 for 27 in MCC's first innings, and 2 for 25 in the second. After this, his name disappears from all match scores. Ahsan had arrived in England as the doors were beginning to close on bowlers with less than erect actions. The law-enforcers may have been anxious to avoid a repetition of the 'Griffin affair' which had made a personal tragedy of a Lord's Test with South Africa two years earlier. Whatever the cause, it would appear that quiet words were had behind the scenes, and the future manager of the Pakistan Test team was returned to base nursing a grudge which, twenty-five years later, was hastening his steps in the direction of Faisalabad.

THE DUBIOUS 'FIRSTS'
OF THE FAISALABAD SERIES

Chris Broad may have established a record for reluctance to leave the crease.

Hearteningly, it was a Pakistani newspaper, *The Nation*, that provided the pithiest summary of Faisalabad and what went before: 'In the aftermath of the series there will emerge only one winner, Hasib Ahsan.

The slow departure of England's
Chris Broad.

With the help of his puppet umpires Hasib has frustrated the England team enough to behave in a manner they seemed incapable of.'

All sorts of grim records seem to have been established during the series. In disbelief at the judgement of umpire Shakeel Khan in the First Test at Lahore, Chris Broad may have set up a Test record for length of time at the crease after being given out. (This author believes he may have witnessed a similar kind of phenomenon at a village cricket match near the A4 in Berkshire – two batsmen at the wicket disputing consecutive 'out' decisions while two incoming batsmen hovered at gully and extra cover.) It is also possible that the gap between Graham Gooch's bat and the ball – a matter of six inches, it is reliably reported – when he was given out caught by Shakoor Rana at Faisalabad may represent a record margin for error. Possibly, too, if the neighbouring fielders are to be believed, Shakoor Rana may have surpassed all other umpiring remonstrances in the strength of his abuse of an England captain. And prior to the incident, Mike Gatting may have created another record in terms of registered dissatisfaction with a Test match's management.

In the heat of the controversy, a consoling word from England manager Peter Lush.

Picture of desolation. England's captain, Mike Gatting, at Faisalabad.

The depressing events of Faisalabad are too recent and perhaps too familiar to require detailed examination here. Yet, with the benefit of hindsight, it does seem that one essential issue was lost sight of in all the heat and dust. In the 'wider interests of the game', the TCCB may have been correct in ordering Mike Gatting to apologize to Shakoor Rana, but this apology should have been conditional upon the restoration of the missing third day. Whether Rana could find a verbal formula to cover his obvious hostility to Gatting and his team was of secondary importance.

In the event, no kind of bargain was struck. The day of 9 December at Faisalabad accordingly disappeared into a void for which cricketing terminology has no description. 'No play' is all *The Cricketer* can manage on its scorecard of the match. Yet the day was, by all accounts, warm and sunny. Test-match playing hours have been restricted by rain, hail, snow, bad light and, in the West Indies and Pakistan, occasionally by rioting. But no day had ever previously been lost due to an umpire's impression that he had been gravely insulted. The result was that England drew a Test match that could have been won, and the series was squared (they had had a lead of 101 on the first innings). From that point onwards the series, as a contest, became meaningless.

It must be said that the TCCB was not the only official body to get its priorities wrong. By refusing to return the missing day, the Pakistan Board handed abundant ammunition to those who were suggesting that the series had been rigged from the start. Surely this was the point at which the England team should have been brought home, leaving Shakoor Rana to claim the dubious distinction of being the first umpire, with no assistance from the weather, to wash out a Test match all on his own.

9
THE FASHION SETTERS

Cricket is not like fashion: its trends change far more slowly. Nevertheless, you only have to thumb through a pictorial history of the game to see that it has come a long way from Hambledon in style alone. It is not known who decided that cricket was best played in a topper, but anyone who has attended a wedding on a windy spring day will concede that it is not the ideal headgear for outdoor sports.

FELIX AND THE CAP (AND GLOVES)

The man who made the break from the 'Ascot opening day' fashion in cricket was the Blackheath schoolmaster Felix (Nicholas Wanostrocht) whom we have already met as a pioneer of the cut. 'I strongly recommend a cap made of chequered woollen,' he wrote in his classic manual *Felix on the Bat*. 'It is light and cool to the head, absorbs perspiration and (which is not an insignificant fact) is not likely to blow off and hit the wicket.' In fact, 'old' George Parr, a captain of the All-England XI, was once given out 'hat hit wicket'.

Just how far Felix was ahead of his contemporaries in terms of practical style is evident from his own watercolour of the All-England XI of 1847. Felix, at manager William Clarke's left elbow, is wearing a topper, as are the vast majority of All-England's stars. Yet a picture of the United All-England XI, painted in 1857, has only one man in a topper.

The All England XI, 1847. Felix, wearing a cap, is seventh from the right.

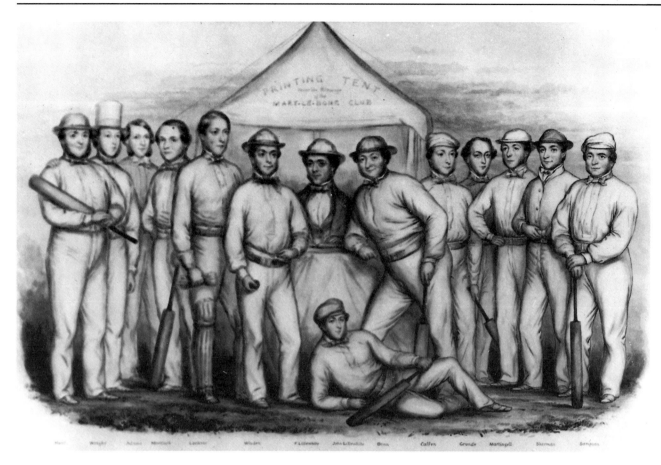

The United Eleven of All England, 1857. Toppers are out, caps and deer stalkers are in.

Some team members have adopted the Felix cap, while still more have adopted a kind of deerstalker which could be regarded as a prototype for the modern cap.

Felix is probably also responsible for removing braces from cricket, long before they became a rarity in the standard male wardrobe. He sensibly advocated an india-rubber belt, 'to do the duty of braces which must be exploded in the active exercise of hitting'.

It is certain that this remarkably versatile and inventive man was a pioneer in protection for batsmen. He created the tubular gloves which, in a modified form, would become standard fashion with W.G. Grace, A.C. MacLaren and others. This significant advance in 'driver safety' was later marketed under patent by the distinguished former umpire William Caldecourt, who does not appear in the previous section simply because no controversy was ever associated with him.

Incidentally, it is interesting to note that gloves were still being discarded as late as 1921. Fuzzy photographs of the action at the Fifth Oval Test show that Warwick Armstrong is wearing only a right-hand glove and that the Australian fast bowler Jack Gregory is not wearing any.

F.P. MILLER – THE PADS PIONEER?

The pioneer of pads is harder to locate. Certainly he was not Kent's Alfred Mynn who, in a North v South match at Leicester, suffered such fearful bruising from Sam Redgate's fast bowling that at one point the doctors considered amputation of his leg. Pads were, however, worn in Mynn's time, though they were a rare and doubtless expensive luxury. My personal candidate for trend-setting in this department is F.P. Miller, the brilliant Surrey batsman and captain who represented his country from 1851 to 1867. In Richard Daft's lavishly illustrated memoirs, *Kings of Cricket*, Miller is the only figure among the faded impressions of players at the wicket who is padded up.

The picture that suggests that F.P. Miller may have pioneered the wearing of pads.

Richard Daft – an early advocate of 'whites'.

RICHARD DAFT OPTS FOR 'WHITES'

Cricket whites – those unmistakable hallmarks that give a county ground or a village green a distinctive magic when play is in progress – have not always been the uniform for the game. And I don't mean simply since the advent of Kerry Packer's pyjama games! Writing near the end of the last century, Richard Daft of All England and Nottinghamshire tells us:

> Coloured shirts were very common in the early part of my time. I have several photographs myself, in which I figure in a striped shirt. Alfred Shaw also appears in a checked shirt of large pattern and dark hue.

The coming of the standard white outfit had social, even spiritual, connotations. Cricket in Richard Daft's youth was a somewhat earthier entertainment than it was to become in later Victorian times. As its management transferred to high-minded patrons with a vision of the game's moral virtues, cricketers started to clothe themselves in the colour of the angels. 'A man on the cricket field looks best in white,' Richard Daft concluded. As a player whose career had stretched from Fuller Pilch to Grace, he was in a unique position to endorse the new trend.

JACK FINGLETON AND THE
BEGINNINGS OF BODY PROTECTION

It was the Bodyline series which taught Test batsmen that pads and gloves were not enough. Jack Fingleton, who scored a brave 83 in the Second Test at Melbourne and bagged a 'pair' at the following Adelaide Test, modelled a bulky suit of padding for an Australian newspaper. He thus introduced an optional form of body protection that would later become essential for batsmen facing Lillee and Thomson, or Holding and Malcolm Marshall. As a top journalist, Fingleton must also have

Early armour and total protection today. Jack Fingleton prepares to face Larwood (this page). Ian Botham gets ready to face the West Indian attack, Trinidad, March 1986 (opposite).

been aware of the propaganda value of these photographs. They graphically illustrated the threat to limb, and possibly life, that Jardine and his men were posing.

THE HELMET PIONEERS

Considering all the thunderbolts that have whizzed around batsmen's ears since Bodyline, the helmet took a surprisingly long time to arrive. Douglas Jardine himself found it convenient to wear a sun helmet during the England *v* India series in the sub-continent in 1933/4. The architect of Bodyline was not exactly helping to further the British image in India, with two fast bowlers, Clark and Nichols, who were striving for Larwood and Voce effects. India, too, had a high-speed merchant in Mahomed Nissar. The bouncers flew from both sides.

In the previous summer in England, the West Indies had given England a sample of what it felt like to be on the receiving end of Bodyline. Walter Hammond's jaw was broken in the Manchester Test,

Patsy Hendren's home-made 'helmet'.

'A batsman ought not to look like an affronted turkey cock.' Mike Brearley faces Jeff Thomson.

though Jardine scored a cool 127 against the packed leg-side field and the high flyers of Constantine and Martindale.

The same attack was responsible for the appearance of the first home-made helmet. 'Patsy' Hendren of Middlesex (and England, of course) walked out to face Constantine and Martindale in Middlesex's match with the tourists at Lord's wearing three caps stitched together so that the peaks protected his ears. Hendren was a comic card, and as such was hugely popular with the Lord's crowds. Laughter greeted him all the way to the crease. But Hendren's original headgear was a serious effort to fashion protection when none was available across the counter. An anxious Mrs H had sat up late over her sewing machine on the eve of the match.

Mike Brearley was the first Test player to wear a helmet in England, but it was not purpose-built. The occasion was the Second Test against Pakistan at Lord's in 1978. The England captain scored a total of 2 in a motorcyclist's crash helmet, to some derision from the media. It was argued that Brearley had no need of such armour in view of the easy pace of Pakistan without Imran, who was signed with Packer, and there was at the same time an instinctive resistance to seeing the accoutrements of American football on the cricket field. Brearley abandoned the crash helmet, but continued his search for effective head protection; he had, after all, the best brain in cricket! He next appeared in a reinforced England cap with plastic ear flaps. This new fashion was also coolly received. 'A batsman ought not to look like an affronted turkey cock,' commented *The Cricketer*.

Left and above: Mike Brearley models a new helmet. He helped to make protective headgear mainstream fashion.

All inventive minds are in line for the scepticism and derision of others. As Fred Astaire and Ginger Rogers sang, 'They all laughed at Christopher Columbus when he said the world was round . . .' But Brearley had the satisfaction of seeing a practical cricket helmet go into full production. Dennis Amiss of England and Edgbaston was one of the first customers, not surprisingly after his hair-raising experiences in Australia against Lillee and Thomson in 1974/5. There is a sad footnote to this purchase, however. In his first Test for England, Warwickshire's left-handed opener Andy Lloyd took a hideous crack on the side of the head from a low bumper delivered by Malcolm Marshall of the West Indies. Lloyd was hospitalized for five days with blurred vision and has yet to regain a Test place. The helmet he was wearing was borrowed from his Warwickshire team-mate, Amiss. The oldest helmet on the county circuit, it had worn too soft for safety against a bowler of Marshall's pace.

Opposite: Sunil Gavaskar's distinctive helmet style. Inset: Dennis Amiss, another helmet pioneer.

Andy Lloyd felled by Malcolm Marshall during the First Test, England *v* West Indies, Edgbaston 1984.

Glen Turner and his heavyweight
bat.

GLENN TURNER AND THE HEAVYWEIGHT BAT

Fashions in bats have changed so rapidly in recent years that one must suspect the influence of sophisticated merchandising rather than batsmen's restlessness for change. One overall fashion trend must be noted, however – the swing towards the heavier blade. Average bat weights increased by 30 per cent in the 1970s. Glenn Turner of New Zealand and Worcestershire weighed in with a Duncan Fearnley of 3 lb 4 oz for his epic innings of 311 not out against Warwickshire at Worcester in 1982. A common theme of all batting instruction books – Ranji's and W.G.'s included – is the danger of investing in too heavy a blade. Yet Turner argued that if a heavy bat is picked up straight, it is less liable to go off line in the execution of the stroke. Clive Lloyd, Ian Botham and Clive Rice are among modern batsmen who have adopted a similar argument – and with Turner that makes a difficult quartet to argue with.

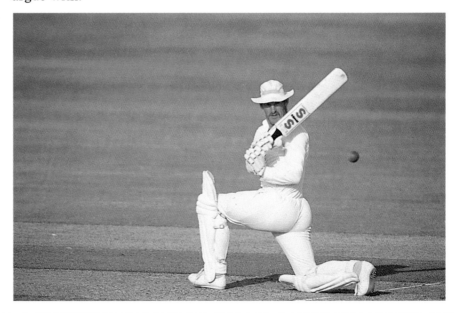

Clive Rice – another batsman to break with orthodoxy in bat weights.

THE
MATCHES

1
THE WORLD TURNS UPSIDE DOWN

As King George III's redcoats filed out of Yorktown to surrender to George Washington's American colonial army, a British regimental band struck up a popular tune of the time with a bitter meaning for England at that hour. The name of the tune was 'The World Turned Upside Down'.

The history of cricket has its own 'Yorktowns' – moments when, to its consternation, the mother country found itself outplayed by colonies (new or old) it had imagined should have been everlastingly grateful for having been taught the game in the first place. Like Yorktown itself, such shattering encounters have tended to benefit England in the long run, and have certainly done wonders for cricket in the victorious countries. Thus, any review of the matches that have changed cricket must give generous space to those that 'turned the world upside down'.

THE INVASION OF THE WICKET-SNATCHERS

The first shock to English cricketing prestige was administered as long ago as 1878 when a party of Australians arrived with little fanfare in the middle of a damp and chilly May. Bearing in mind the travelling time

Victorious strangers – the Australians in England 1878.

J. BLACKHAM   T. HORAN.   G H. BAILEY.   D. W. GREGORY   J. CONWAY   A. BANNERMAN.   C BANNERMAN.   W. L. MURDOCH.
F. R. SPOFFORTH.   F. ALLAN.   W. MIDWINTER.   T. W. GARRETT.   H. F. BOYLE.

W.G. Grace – 4 and 0 in his first meeting with the Australians.

involved and England's hazy knowledge of its new colony, they could as well have been visitors from Outer Mongolia. There was certainly no question of awarding the tourists a Test match, but a game against an MCC team at Lord's was granted. Before this match the visitors, dressed in inappropriate silk shirts, went down to an innings defeat at Nottingham in inhospitable weather conditions.

The sun was showing no sign of appearing when the Australians arrived by horse carriage at Lord's on the morning of 27 May. There had been heavy overnight rain and puddles were still lying in the outfield. Only 500 spectators had turned up to see these strangers play. The MCC was not quite at Test strength; indeed, a Test match had yet to be played in England. However, the opening pair alone was formidable – W.G. Grace, who probably required no introduction, and the brilliant A.N. Hornby, Lancashire's captain and batting stay.

The match was not five minutes old before Grace was back in the pavilion, caught at square leg for 4. He was shortly followed by Cambridge University's Clement Booth, bowled for a duck. In under an hour, MCC were all out for 33. The Nottinghamshire pair of Alfred Shaw and Fred Morley immediately struck back. The Australians were dismissed for 41, a lead of only 8. All could yet be saved.

At 4 p.m., the MCC began its second innings to excited cheering. The word had got around that strange things were happening at Lord's. A group of 500 had swollen to a crowd of 5000. Cheers turned to an astonished roar as Grace was missed first ball behind the wicket. Then the volume increased as Spofforth's second ball made the bails fly. Spofforth's third ball disposed of A.J. Webbe in similar fashion. At the other end, Boyle clean bowled Booth and Ridley in his first over. Hornby had indicated he might be beginning to get the measure of this other-worldly bowling in his first innings knock of 19; but now he was struck a blow from Spofforth which some would contend was to leave a permanent scar on his batting. MCC were all out for a humiliating total of 19 soon after five o'clock. By twenty minutes to six, with over a day

MCC *v* THE AUSTRALIANS, 1878

Played at Lord's, 27 May
Result: The Australians won by nine wickets

MCC

W.G. Grace, c Midwinter, b Allan	4	b Spofforth	0
A.N. Hornby, b Spofforth	19	b Boyle	1
C. Booth, b Boyle	0	b Boyle	0
A.W. Ridley, c A. Bannerman, b Boyle	7	b Boyle	0
A.J. Webbe, b Spofforth	1	b Spofforth	0
F. Wyld, b Boyle	0	b Boyle	5
W. Flowers, c and b Spofforth	0	b Boyle	11
G.G. Hearne, b Spofforth	0	b Spofforth	0
A. Shaw, st Murdoch, b Spofforth	0	not out	2
G.F. Vernon, st Murdoch, b Spofforth	0	b Spofforth	0
F. Morley, not out	1	c Horan, b Boyle	0
l-b	1		
Total	**33**	**Total**	**19**

THE AUSTRALIANS

C. Bannerman, c Hearne, b Morley	0	b Shaw	1
W. Midwinter, c Wyld, b Shaw	10	not out	4
T. Horan, c Grace, b Morley	4	not out	7
A.C. Bannerman, c Booth, b Morley	0		
T.W. Garrett, c Ridley, b Morley	6		
F.R. Spofforth, b Shaw	1		
D.W. Gregory, b Shaw	0		
H.F. Boyle, c Wyld, b Morley	2		
W.L. Murdoch, b Shaw	9		
F.E. Allan, c and b Shaw	6		
G.H. Bailey, not out	3		
Total	**41**	**Total (1 wkt)**	**12**

BOWLING ANALYSIS

THE AUSTRALIANS

	O	M	R	W		O	M	R	W
Boyle	14	7	14	3	Boyle	8.1	6	3	6
Spofforth	5.3	3	4	6	Spofforth	9	2	16	4
Allan	9	4	14	1					

MCC

	O	M	R	W		O	M	R	W
Shaw	33.2	25	10	5	Shaw	8	6	4	1
Morley	33	19	31	5	Morley	8	4	8	0

Umpires: A. Rylott and M. Sherwin

The 'demon' Spofforth taught the Mother Country some valuable cricket lessons.

left for play, the Australians had made the 12 runs necessary for victory. It is reported that at Covent Garden a crowd formed outside the Tavistock Hotel where the visitors were staying – Londoners anxious to see what manner of men had done this thing.

The Australians' batting was nothing to write home about, as is evident from the remarkable scorecard of the Lord's encounter. But the team had four sensational pace bowlers in Allan, Garrett, Boyle and the 'Demon', Spofforth. Allan may have anticipated John Barton King in his ability to make the ball 'swerve', a movement he obtained with a peculiar knee-jerk. The others could be described as fast spinners. A photograph of Spofforth, who was to torment English batsmen in many

The 1878 Australians *v* Thornton's XI. Note the close fielder on the leg.

Tests to come, shows him contorted from the effort of bowling a fast leg-break. Certainly contemporary English batting was quite unprepared for this form of attack, having for some years been lulled into unhurried stroke-play against medium-pace bowling in the Alfred Shaw style.

In a way, the overthrow of the MCC in 1878 had more profound effects on English cricket than the more celebrated defeat at The Oval four years later, though admittedly the latter set up the Ashes contest. The disaster of 1878 resulted in immediate changes in English cricketing methodology. County sides were taught the value of an alert, attacking field – a close fielder on the leg side was a novelty to English eyes. Again, it seems that county captains had never considered setting fields for individual bowlers. Now they did. Finally, it was noted that medium pace, however accurate, was not enough. The search began for fast bowlers who could beat Australia.

RAMADHIN'S AND VALENTINE'S DAY

In retrospect it is hard to understand why the result of the Second Test at Lord's in June 1950 came as such a shock to England's supporters. It goes without saying that England has gained plenty of experience of being beaten by West Indies since that date; but even before then there had been conclusive defeats in the Caribbean. As recently as 1947/8, a team led by G.O. Allen had lost a West Indies series by nil to two. However, it was argued that England in the West Indies had never been at fully representative strength. These were times before the fear of defection to 'breakaway' touring ventures forced the authorities to cram the calendar with full-strength Test tours. Besides, the West Indies had so far to win a single Test in England. Yet it must have been evident to anyone who had troubled to read the reports of the 1947/8 tour that in Worrell, Weekes and Walcott the visitors had a trio of batsmen who could not be dismissed lightly.

Frank Worrell of the 'Three Ws'. England should have been warned.

G.O. Allen in 1937. Post-war his team would suffer a 2–0 defeat in West Indies.

Possibly the shock was due to a feeling, prevalent earlier in the summer, that England's Test fortunes at home were due for a revival after a humiliating defeat by Australia in 1948 and a drawn series with New Zealand in 1949. The optimists pointed to Fenners, where four Cambridge undergraduates – Messrs J.G. Dewes, D.S. Sheppard, G.H.G. Doggart and P.B.H. May – were performing batting marvels. Indeed, the prolific four were jointly to amass 524 runs out of a Cambridge total of 594 for 4 wickets declared against John Goddard's West Indian tourists in mid May.

Indeed, the West Indians' early efforts, in weather conditions similar to those faced by the Australians in 1878, were patronizingly regarded. A three-wicket victory over Yorkshire was written off as a near defeat, and serious lapses in the field were noted. 'Possibly the warm weather will bring an improvement,' *The Cricketer* suggested. Then England won the First Test at Manchester by 202 runs on a wicket that might have been made for the West Indies' two young spinners, Sonny

Ramadhin and Alf Valentine. No small advantage in a four-match series.

And so to Lord's on Thursday 24 June: glorious weather, a firm, true wicket and West Indies' powerful batting line-up restricted to what in the circumstances could be regarded from an England point of view as a reasonable 320 for 7. The tail was wrapped up next morning for the addition of only 6 runs. The second day was warm and sunny too, but it turned out to be one of the greyest of all days for English batting. This was a West Indies attack that worked on a totally different principle to that which is now favoured. A fastish bowler caller Prior Jones, with Frank Worrell in support, sent down the minimum number of overs required to remove the gloss from the new ball. Then the spinners came on, in this case for the most part of the innings.

Hutton and Washbrook began with their customary confidence. But with the score at 62 for 0, Hutton now uncharacteristically charged the left-arm spinner Alf Valentine and was stumped by yards. Twelve runs later, Washbrook was stumped off Ramadhin, a decision requiring no replay even had the facility existed. Bill Edrich hung on grimly, so grimly that his partners became paralysed. The young hope, Doggart of Cambridge, departed for 0 as did another young batsman of whom great things were expected, Gilbert Parkhouse of Glamorgan. Meanwhile, Edrich's painstaking score of 8 was to cost him his Test place for over three years. Only an abrasive counter-attack by Yorkshire's Johnny Wardle provided a contrast to a story of total mesmerization. On a golden evening, suburban trains were filled with men with binoculars, staring vacantly ahead of them. England were all out for 151.

The West Indians went on to rub home the advantage with a second

The terrible twins – Sonny Ramadhin and Alf Valentine.

innings of 425 for 6 declared. The heftiest and hardest hitting of the 'Three Ws', Clive Walcott, felt encouraged to cut loose with an innings of 168 not out. This was humiliation on a Bradman-like scale. But there was a significant difference; these dark days for England were lightened by an unprecedented manifestation of gaiety, colour, wit and song. England's new West Indian community virtually monopolized the Nursery End. All this added a refreshing new dimension to a Lord's Test match. St John's Wood crowds had hitherto taken their pleasures more sombrely, in terms of both dress and apparent involvement.

Cyril Washbrook made a sturdy century in England's second innings, but Sonny Ramadhin and Alf Valentine steadily deprived him of partners until the moment arrived for an inevitable and jubilant pitch invasion shortly after lunch on the final day. Steel drums hammered home the fact that, after twenty years of Test playing, the West Indies

Sonny Ramadhin bowling in a 1950 practice match. Later he would put England in a spin.

Alf Valentine hides his spinning secret.

had finally triumphed in England, and by a margin of 326 runs! England had been outplayed in every department, not least in fielding (warm weather had indeed brought an improvement); but the special heroes of the hour were, in the words of Lord Bergner's famous calypso, 'those two little pals of mine – Ramadhin and Valentine'.

Ramadhin was only twenty years old in 1950 and had played a mere handful of first-class games before selection for the tour. Yet he posed problems as baffling at the time as those now flighted by Pakistan's Abdul Qadir. A magic finger action made it difficult to tell his off-break from his leg-break. Waiting to see which way the ball bounced, legions of England and county batsmen perished.

Alfred L. Valentine was a year younger, and even less experienced. In only two previous first-class games he had obtained figures of 2 for 190. 'One might wonder why he is going to England,' a Caribbean

ENGLAND *v* WEST INDIES, 1950

Second Test match played at Lord's, 24, 25, 26, 28, 29 June
Result: West Indies won by 326 runs

WEST INDIES

A.F. Rae, c and b Jenkins	106	b Jenkins	24
J.B. Stollmeyer, lbw b Wardle	20	b Jenkins	30
F.M. Worrell, b Bedser	52	c Doggart, b Jenkins	45
E. Weekes, b Bedser	63	run out	63
C.L. Walcott, st Evans, b Jenkins	14	not out	168
G.E. Gomez, st Evans, b Jenkins	1	c Edrich, b Bedser	70
R.J. Christiani, b Bedser	33	not out	5
J.D.C. Goddard (capt), b Wardle	14	c Evans, b Jenkins	11
P.E. Jones, c Evans, b Jenkins	0		
S. Ramadhin, not out	1		
A. Valentine, c. Hutton, b Jenkins	5		
B 10, l-b 5, w 1, n-b 1	17	l-b 8, n-b 1	9
Total	326	Total (6 wkts dec)	425

Fall of wickets. First innings: 1–37, 2–128, 3–233, 4–262, 5–273, 6–274, 7–320, 8–320, 9–320. Second innings: 1–48, 2–75, 3–108, 4–146, 5–199, 6–410.

ENGLAND

L. Hutton, st Walcott, b Valentine	35	b Valentine	10
C. Washbrook, st Walcott, b Ramadhin	36	b Ramadhin	114
W.J. Edrich, c Walcott, b Ramadhin	8	c Jones, b Ramadhin	8
G.H.G. Doggart, lbw b Ramadhin	0	b Ramadhin	25
W.G.A. Parkhouse, b Valentine	0	c Goddard, b Valentine	48
N.W.D. Yardley (capt), b Valentine	16	c Weekes, b Valentine	19
T.G. Evans, b Ramadhin	8	c Rae, b Ramadhin	2
R.O. Jenkins, c Walcott, b Valentine	4	b Ramadhin	4
J.H. Wardle, not out	33	lbw b Worrell	21
A.V. Bedser, b Ramadhin	8	b Ramadhin	0
R. Berry, c Goddard, b Jones	2	not out	0
B 2, l-b 1, w 1	4	B 16, l-b 7	23
Total	151	Total	274

Fall of wickets. First innings: 1–62, 2–74, 3–74, 4–75, 5–86, 6–102, 7–110, 8–113, 9–122. Second innings: 1–26, 2–57, 3–140, 4–218, 5–228, 6–238, 7–245, 8–258, 9–258.

BOWLING ANALYSIS

ENGLAND

	O	M	R	W		O	M	R	W
Bedser	40	14	60	3	Bedser	44	16	80	1
Edrich	16	4	30	0	Edrich	13	2	37	0
Jenkins	35.2	6	116	5	Jenkins	59	13	174	4
Wardle	17	6	46	2	Wardle	30	10	58	0
Berry	19	7	45	0	Berry	32	15	67	0
Yardley	4	1	12	0					

WEST INDIES

	O	M	R	W		O	M	R	W
Jones	8.4	2	13	1	Jones	7	1	22	0
Worrell	10	4	20	0	Worrell	22.3	9	39	1
Valentine	45	28	48	4	Valentine	71	47	79	3
Ramadhin	43	27	66	5	Ramadhin	72	43	86	6
					Gomez	13	1	25	0
					Goddard	6	6	0	0

Umpires: D. Davies and F.S. Lee

correspondent wrote before the season began. But the trigger action of Valentine's left thumb allowed few lucky breaks to batsmen that summer.

Jubilant West Indian supporters acclaim a famous victory.

Many results flowed from this famous victory, among them a surge of confidence and pride in the West Indies and a great fillip for the young West Indian community in London. But the major benefactor was Test cricket itself. Up until now there had been a tendency to regard England *v* Australia as the only true Test, which to this way of thinking meant that a 'true Test' series came round only every four years. Now international cricket became a genuine 'three-ring' contest. Moreover, never again would the West Indies be regarded as unworthy of a full five-Test programme, especially after Goddard's men went on to win the remaining two Tests in the 1950 series by margins of 10 wickets and an innings and 56 runs.

BIRTH OF A TEST NATION

England's cricket administrators deplored the partition of India in 1947. Even as a unified dominion India had hardly been able to mount a genuine challenge in English conditions. Now here was this new nation, Pakistan, clamouring for its rightful place on the Test circuit, though geographically it constituted less than half of India and, in terms of talent, could claim only one class player from the all-India team of 1946 – her captain, A.H. Kardar, formerly Abdul Hafeez.

Nothing much in the way of contest and excitement was therefore expected from the Pakistanis in their first tour of England in 1954. The visitors were allotted four Test matches – generous in the circumstances, it was felt. Events seemed, at first, to bear this suspicion out. Only rain (three solid days of it) saved Pakistan from ignominious defeat in the First Test at Lord's. The tour had coincided with one of the wettest summers on record. For the Second Test at Trent Bridge the weather improved sufficiently to reveal the true difference between the two teams, at least in the view of England supporters. England won by an innings and 129 runs. Denis Compton climbed into a time

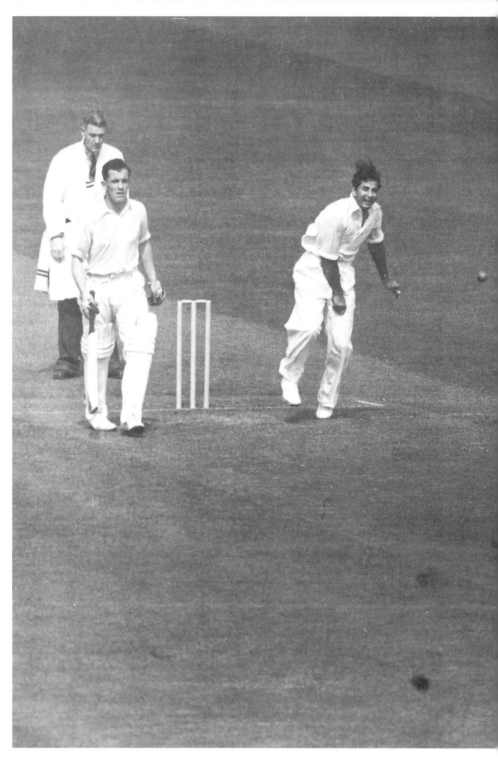

machine to return to his rumbustious form of 1947, scoring 278 in 290 minutes. Pakistan's outfield wilted under his hammer blows. Dependable throwing arms proved as scarce as safe pairs of hands. Rain robbed England of certain victory at Manchester – England 359 for 9 declared, Pakistan 90 and 25 for 4 wickets.

The Fourth Test at The Oval looked like a formality, always provided that it was not washed out by the summer's atrocious weather. On this assumption, the selectors decided to rest Alec Bedser and Trevor Bailey and blood two youngsters earmarked for the Australian tour, Frank Tyson and Peter Loader. This was perhaps an enterprising decision, but it stripped the team of balance as well as 'seam' ability. Wicket-keeper Godfrey Evans, a pugnacious 'do or die' number seven or eight, was promoted to unaccustomed responsibility at number six.

England's conqueror Fazal
Mahmood at the crease.

Hutton, though badly out of form as a result of a gruelling West Indies tour the previous winter, returned as captain and opener. In his absence the selectors had been flirting with David Sheppard as a possible replacement captain.

Pakistan won the toss and was bundled out for 133, no real departure from the form the team had shown all season. No play was possible on the second day; but the sun returned on Saturday to complicate a rain-damaged pitch. An England team that included Hutton, Simpson, May, Compton and Graveney found itself all out for 130. Spectators were kept busy pencilling in the name Fazal on their scorecards as the successful bowler. In fact, Fazal Mahmood took 6 England wickets for 53.

Hutton now urged his bowlers into all-out attack. Such was the

Match summary: Pakistan first innings: 133 (A.H. Kardar 36, Tyson 4 wickets 35 runs). England first innings: 130 (T.W. Graveney 53, Fazal Mahmood 6 wickets 53 runs). Pakistan second innings: 164 (Wazir Mohammad 42 no, Wardle 7 wickets 56 runs). England second innings: 143 (P.B.H. May 53, Fazal Mahmood 6 wickets 46 runs). Result: Pakistan won by 24 runs.

response that Pakistan had soon lost 8 wickets for 82. Now history began to enter the match. Inspired by Wazir Mohammad, the last two Pakistan wickets precisely doubled the score of the previous eight. Pakistan were all out for 164. The result still seemed a formality: England had a day and two and a half hours to score the necessary 168 runs for victory. Perhaps there was almost too much time; the prospect of a full rest day may have seemed hard to resist. Besides, there was always the possibility that rain would intervene on the morrow. Hutton decided to try to finish things off that Monday evening.

Hutton himself went for 5 runs, looking to set an example for haste. Simpson, May and Compton continued the assault policy with more success. When the fourth wicket fell there were 109 runs on the board. Then, in a radical attempt to accelerate the tempo, Hutton promoted the already over-elevated Godfrey Evans to Tom Graveney's spot at number five. Evans scored 3 and Graveney, with his confidence sapped, made 0. England finished the day at 124 for 6 wickets. The result was no longer a formality, though 40 runs from the last four English wickets was not an impossible demand. As it happened, only 19 runs were scored next morning before a sharp return from Hanif Mohammad ran out McConnon and terminated the short story of England's long tail. As in the first innings, Fazal took 6 wickets, this time for 46.

Fazal Mahmood was a brilliant medium-pace bowler in the Bedser

Demon bowler Fazal Mahmood in an uncharacteristic role.

mould who, like the great Alec, thrived in humid conditions, as indeed did England's missing all-rounder Trevor Bailey. The essential difference between the two teams was that England left out Bedser, leaving Pakistan with the bowler best able to exploit the conditions obtaining at The Oval in mid August 1954. It was a mistake that was to bring about the birth of a Test nation.

Pitch invasion. A dog hurries to congratulate Sunil Gavaskar. Keith Fletcher, Richard Hutton and Alan Knott are the fielders. Later an elephant would put in an appearance.

INDIAN SUMMER

India had to wait seventeen more years to win her first Test in England; but when her hour came she was to slay two dragons within the space of nine months. In the winter prior to her 1971 England tour she accomplished the spectacular feat of beating the West Indies on their home ground.

Yet India's three-Test tour of 1971 had remarkable similarities to the Pakistan tour of 1954. Rain robbed England of victory at Manchester, and possibly at Lord's. So to The Oval, once again shrouded by low-lying cloud. England's first innings of 353, built from solid contributions by Jameson, Richard Hutton and Alan Knott, looked like a safe if not a winning total. It looked even better when India were dismissed for 284, captain Ray Illingworth being the leading wicket-taker with 5 for 70. Then Monday-morning blues afflicted England and, perhaps more to the point, so did the leg-spin of Bhagwat Chandrasekhar, 'Chandra' for short, supported by S. Venkat.

Chandra's triumph over England that grey Monday was also a personal victory over many adversities. He was virtually a one-armed cricketer, one arm having been paralysed since childhood. Moreover,

Chandra (left) and India's captain
Wadekar savour the triumph.

Chandra was not always able to strike the length he hit upon on Monday 24 August 1971. He had been so roughly handled by Australian batsmen in 1967/8 that he had lost his Test place. Then a scooter accident seemed to deny him all chance of regaining it. He had played no part in India's triumph over the West Indies that winter. Indeed, Chandra could be said to have been lucky to be in a position to seize the historic opportunity that a relenting fate now held out for him.

The wicket was not remarkably helpful, though it offered the kind of encouragement a spinner hopes to find on a fourth-day track. The big advantage that Chandra had going for him was the English batsmen's total unfamiliarity with, and suspicion of, well directed leg-spin. By the tea interval England were all out for 101. Chandra took 6 wickets for 38 – similar but slightly better figures than Fazal's in his famous Oval spell back in 1954.

John Snow now picked up the gauntlet and trapped Sunil Gavaskar lbw for 0. Derek Underwood had A.V. Mankad caught for 11. Two wickets were down for 37; but the score had crept to 76 without further loss by close of play.

The next morning Underwood accounted for Sardesai and Solkar, and a quicksilver effort by Alan Knott ran out Indian captain Wadekar for 45. With 5 wickets down for 135 and 38 needed to win, there was still a chance that England could snatch victory against lower-order batsmen with a momentous responsibility on their shoulders. But the sixth wicket did not fall until 170 had been put on the board. India now needed only 3 runs to win, and this Engineer accomplished with a boundary. In the closing stages of the day, an elephant in Indian colours (though a resident of Chessington Zoo) was paraded on The Oval square. This was certainly a victory India would never forget.

In 1983 at Leeds, New Zealand became the last of the pre-war Test nations to beat England in the lion's den. It was the beginning of an era in which England would find it hard to beat anyone on home wickets.

2
TALES OF
THE UNEXPECTED

'You never can tell in this game of cricket' is a well-worn cliché of the commentary box. As it happens, quite often we *can* tell the likely result of a Test on the first evening; as, for example, when West Indies have 360 for 4 on the board, and England have still to bat. Yet there have been games which have seen almost miraculous reversals of fortune, and as such have gained new stature and popularity for cricket. It is possible that before Headingley 1981 there were some people living in England who had never heard of Ian Botham; after this epic Test they must have been limited to babes in arms.

It is certain, too, that it is the great 'fight backs' that live longest in folk memory. The story of Jessop's innings in the 1902 Oval game is one that has been handed down from father to son along, perhaps, with tales of Waterloo and the Battle of Britain, rekindling new enthusiasm for the game with each generation. For all these reasons, the cricket matches that upset all the odds (Dennis Lillee, it will be remembered, got odds of 100 to 1 at Headingley in 1981) must come into the reckoning as games that have changed cricket to its lasting benefit.

ENGLAND'S FINEST HOURS

Two Test matches stand out among the thousands played where total capitulation appeared to be the obvious course, but some instinct that hated inevitability brought about a surprise ending. Though there are clearly other contenders, England *v* Australia at The Oval in 1902 and England *v* Australia at Headingley in 1981 are the perfect illustrations of the triumph of the 'never-say-die' attitude.

Though widely separated in time, there are many similarities between the two Tests. The players who reported to The Oval in August 1902 were still smarting from defeat by 3 runs at the previous Manchester Test which, but for a crucially dropped catch by Fred Tate of Sussex and the wretched man's failure to stay put whilst Rhodes knocked off the necessary three runs, should have squared the rubber for England. Headingley in 1981 had a similarly bleak background: defeat at Trent Bridge and the worst of a draw at Lord's which, incidentally, had cost the man of the hour, Ian Botham, the England captaincy. But there was a difference. A.C. MacLaren's men, two down at The Oval, could only hope to redeem something of England's honour. Brearley's team at Leeds still had everything to play for.

At The Oval at close of play on Monday 11 August 1902, it looked as if even hopes of redeemed national honour were slipping away. Thanks to Yorkshire's all-rounder George Hirst, Australia were 4 wickets down for 82. But these Ashes winners batted in depth. Hopkins, Trumble and Kelly put on 149 for the eighth and ninth wickets, and the Australian innings closed at 324.

Then the rains came. One can picture England's skipper, Archie MacLaren on this Tuesday morning. The rain left a responsive wicket doleful eyes and drooping moustache. MacLaren was a man inclined to

A.C. MacLaren out to salvage national honour.

Opposite: A photo report of a famous match from the *Illustrated London News*.

think that fate and heaven had a grudge against him. 'My God, look what they've sent me!' he had exclaimed as England's curious selections for the previous Test had arrived at Old Trafford – a mournful outburst that conceivably indicated that he believed this Test lost before a ball was bowled. It surely seemed as if fate was determined to thwart MacLaren on this Tuesday morning. The rain left a responsive wicket for Hugh Trumble's medium-pace spinners and the left-arm slows of John Saunders. England had only six overs' batting before the rain returned to improve conditions still further for the spinners. England were all out at 3.30 for 183. An aggressive knock by George Hirst, like Jessop inexplicably omitted from the Manchester Test, saved MacLaren's men from the ignominy of following on.

Now came the first intimation that the wheel of fortune was not hopelessly spinning in Australia's favour. Victor Trumper made the mistake of attempting a run to Jessop at cover-point, perhaps the world's finest fielder in this position. Trumper's partner, R.A. Duff, knew his man better; he stood his ground. Trumper turned for home, slipped and was run out by yards. England's fielding was remotivated, as were her strike bowler Lockwood and the leg-spinner Braund. Australia were 114 for 8 at close of play and all out for 121 next morning. Yet the statistics of victory were still formidable. England needed 263 to win on a steadily deteriorating batting surface.

It was at this stage of the game that the odds against an England victory really began to stack up. Saunders bowled MacLaren, Palairet and Tyldesley for 2, 6 and 0 respectively. Then he had Surrey's Tom Hayward caught by wicket-keeper Kelly for 7. The fifth wicket fell with only 48 runs on the board.

One might say that Gilbert Jessop's feelings as he walked to the wicket can only be imagined, but in fact we do know something of them. Added to the tensions of the moment were 'uncomfortable' (his word) recollections of the previous evening's events at the Central London Hotel where, over a bottle of 'Pommery' or two, he had been moved to open a book on his forthcoming innings. The punters had been invited to put their money on a Jessop fifty or the longer shot of a century. With England's score standing at 48 for 5, he was now bitterly regretting his bravado.

At the same time, Jessop wanted a big innings for personal as well as patriotic reasons. Just as Walter Read's demotion to number ten in the order had encouraged him to 'show them' at The Oval eighteen years earlier, so Jessop's omission from the previous Manchester Test still rankled, understandably considering he had scored a spectacular 55 out of a miserable England total in the Third, Sheffield, Test. Indeed, one wag had suggested that the selectors must have lost his address. (Again at Headingley in 1981, we find Ian Botham smarting from his dismissal/resignation from the England captaincy. Is it a coincidence that the great 'fight backs' of Test cricket have been led by men with a point to prove?)

The Australians, however, were not to know the various thoughts that were passing through Gilbert Jessop's mind; they knew only that he had taken 7 runs off Saunders' first over to him and that now he had landed a six off Trumble on the pavilion awnings. 'Why in the name of sense can't he go steady for a bit?' cried a Surrey member sitting in its shade. 'He'll slog a few more then they'll catch him in the deep!' The next moment Jessop came dancing down the wicket for a repeat performance and missed. Unaccountably keeper Kelly fumbled a crucial stumping chance. The whole Oval circumference started to echo the Surrey member's misgivings, especially when, minutes later, the unlucky Victor Trumper dropped a searing drive at long-off.

After lunch, with partner F.S. Jackson in an untypical sheet-anchor role, Jessop tore into the Australian attack like the hurricane his mood

TEST MATCH.

1. R. A. Duff and C. V. Trumper open the Australian innings.   2. A. C. MacLaren, the English Captain.   3. J. Darling, the Australian Captain.   4. George Hirst bowling to Noble.   5. England leaves the field.   6. H. Trumble, 64 not out.

of the morning had clearly forecasted. Saunders, Trumble, Noble and Warwick Armstrong were no longer eager volunteers for bowling service. Yet in the outfield there was no hiding place from Jessop's bruising cuts, drives, sweeps and pulls. Once again, comparisons with Botham at Headingley immediately suggest themselves; yet it would be wrong to picture a similar figure at the wicket. The 'Croucher' Jessop was a short, stocky man who, true to his sobriquet, bent low over his bat and came at the bowler as if released by a spring mechanism. Jessop also had a unique and convoluted grip, at the base of the bat handle, that added an extra unpredictability to his stroke-play. Aggression the two men certainly shared, as well as the rare distinction of completely demolishing a winning Australian attack. In an hour Jessop had added 75 runs to bring the England total to 109 for 5. For the first time in the match the crowd sensed the possibility, albeit a distant one, of an England victory. Hansom cabs began to clatter across Westminster Bridge – the passengers no doubt urging on the drivers with promises of additional gold if they could make The Oval while Jessop was still batting.

With the score at 157, Jackson was caught and bowled by Trumble for a restrained yet invaluable 49. Now, with the entrance of George Hirst, the two Old Trafford rejects were at the wicket. Jessop welcomed his partner with neglect, with two boundaries off Trumble and a couple of comfortably run twos. Then he swept Armstrong for four to bring up his century and immediately repeated the performance. Attempting yet

Gilbert Jessop came at the bowler as if released from a spring.

ENGLAND *v* AUSTRALIA, 1902

Fifth Test match played at The Oval, 11–13 August
Result: England won by 1 wicket

AUSTRALIA

R.A. Duff, c Lilley, b Hirst	23	b Lockwood	6
V.T. Trumper, b Hirst	42	run out	2
C. Hill, b Hirst	11	c MacLaren, b Hirst	34
J. Darling (capt), c Lilley, b Hirst	3	c MacLaren, b Lockwood	15
M.A. Noble, c and b Jackson	52	b Braund	13
S.E. Gregory, b Hirst	23	b Braund	9
W.W. Armstrong, b Jackson	17	b Lockwood	21
A.J. Hopkins, c MacLaren, b Lockwood	40	c Lilley, b Lockwood	3
H. Trumble, not out	64	not out	7
J.J. Kelly, c Rhodes, b Braund	39	lbw b Lockwood	0
J.V. Saunders, lbw b Braund	0	c Tyldesley, b Rhodes	2
B 5, l-b 3, n-b 2	10	B 7, l-b 2	9
Total	324	Total	121

Fall of wickets. First innings: 1–47, 2–63, 3–82, 4–82, 5–126, 6–174, 7–175, 8–256, 9–324, 10–324. Second innings: 1–6, 2–9, 3–31, 4–71, 5–75, 6–91, 7–95, 8–114, 9–115, 10–121.

ENGLAND

A.C. MacLaren (capt), c Armstrong, b Trumble	10	b Saunders	2
L.C. Palairet, b Trumble	20	b Saunders	6
J.T. Tyldesley, b Trumble	33	b Saunders	0
T. Hayward, b Trumble	0	c Kelly, b Saunders	7
F.S. Jackson, c Armstrong, b Saunders	2	c and b Trumble	49
L.C. Braund, c Hill, b Trumble	22	c Kelly, b Trumble	2
G.L. Jessop, b Trumble	13	c Noble b Armstrong	104
G.H. Hirst, c and b Trumble	43	not out	58
W.H. Lockwood, c Noble, b Saunders	25	lbw b Trumble	2
A.A. Lilley, c Trumper, b Trumble	0	c Darling, b Trumble	16
W. Rhodes, not out	0	not out	6
B 13, l-b 2	15	B 5, l-b 6	11
Total	183	Total (9 wkts)	263

Fall of wickets. First innings: 1–31, 2–36, 3–63, 4–67, 5–67, 6–83, 7–137, 8–179, 9–183, 10–183. Second innings: 1–5, 2–5, 3–10, 4–31, 5–48, 6–157, 7–187, 8–214, 9–248.

BOWLING ANALYSIS

ENGLAND

	O	M	R	W		O	M	R	W
Lockwood	24	2	85	1	Lockwood	20	6	45	5
Rhodes	28	9	46	0	Rhodes	22	7	38	1
Hirst	29	5	77	5	Hirst	5	1	7	1
Braund	16.5	5	29	2	Braund	9	1	15	2
Jackson	20	4	66	2	Jackson	4	3	7	0
Jessop	6	2	11	0					

Lockwood, 1 n-b
Rhodes, 1 n-b

AUSTRALIA

	O	M	R	W		O	M	R	W
Trumble	31	13	65	8	Trumble	33.5	4	108	4
Saunders	23	7	79	2	Saunders	24	3	105	4
Noble	7	3	24	0	Noble	5	0	11	0
					Armstrong	4	0	28	1

Umpires: C.E. Richardson and A.A. White

another reprise he dollied to Noble at short-leg. In 139 minutes Jessop had scored 104 runs. The Australian enemy cheered him all the way back to the pavilion, where scenes of fervour awaited him. But when the shouting died down, it was noted that England still needed 76 runs from the last three wickets.

The rest is a story of Yorkshire aggression and grit. Hirst attacked the bowling as if inspired by Jessop, or goaded by the blindness of selectors. But with Lockwood and Lilley departed, and Rhodes slowly making his way to the wicket, 15 runs were still needed for victory – a marathon in circumstances where numbing tension emanated from every corner of the ground. Hirst decided on a fundamental change of tactics: there would be no more swings for the boundary. As every child now knows, or should, they 'got them in singles' with the odd two or three for luck.

'AND YESTERDAY THEY

WERE BURYING ENGLISH CRICKET'

Can you honestly say that if you had had a ticket for the Monday of the Third Test at Leeds, 20 July 1981, you would have hurried out to Headingley? Would you have bothered even to turn up?

Let us briefly remind ourselves how things stood on the Saturday evening. Australia had a first innings total of 401. England had scored 174, failing by 21 runs to save the follow-on. In her second innings, England had lost the wicket of Gooch for 4 runs. Judging by England's form so far, the Test would be finished about tea-time.

There must have been men and women living around Leeds, and perhaps further afield, who calculated along these lines, and to their eternal regret missed the Test day of a lifetime. Possibly one or two of these faint-hearts had access to a TV set, in which case they would have seen nothing in the morning's session to suggest that their lack of faith had been misplaced. Brearley went for 14; David Gower for 9 to another

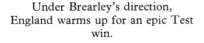

Under Brearley's direction, England warms up for an epic Test win.

A victory against all the odds! How they stood on Saturday evening.

slash into the slips. Gatting with sorrowful disbelief (but no dissension) departed, lbw again, for 1. Only Geoffrey Boycott's straight bat might have prodded the absentee viewer into a mild sense of guilt. The great Yorkshireman on his home ground showed every intention of staying at the wicket until the Tuesday evening. He was joined by Peter Willey, who outlined a less classical method of dealing with the lifting ball – this was no docile fourth-day track. He decided to lift it a little further over the heads of the massed slips; anything shorter he swatted through the covers. Even so, the man with the unused ticket in his pocket would have been correct in thinking that it couldn't last. Hughes moved Dyson to a kind of deep gully to snatch down a Willey high-flyer. England's fight back became, in reality, a matter of 133 for 6, still 94 runs short of the first goal, which was to make Australia bat again.

Headingley was never intended to be Ian Botham's Test. Rodney Marsh might have been excused for thinking it was his own when in the first innings he caught Botham off Lillee to establish a world wicket-keeping record. Dennis Lillee might also have been forgiven for thinking it was his party when, with the capture of Peter Willey's wicket, he overhauled Hugh Trumble's record 141 wickets to become the most successful bowler in Anglo-Australian Tests. The Australian captain, Kim Hughes, could have been pardoned for supposing, at least until late on the Monday evening, that this was the Test where he would finally establish himself securely on the uneasy throne of the Chappell brothers. Even umpires Meyer and Evans might just have imagined that it was they who had made the Test-match news when on the Saturday evening they stopped play for 'bad light' in sunlight and provoked the 'cushion-throwing' incident. In fact, all these milestones and aspirations were to be swept aside by a man who had just lost the England captaincy, and his form for a good many Tests longer.

Yet it had already been noted that Botham was playing like a man released from care. In Australia's first innings he had taken 5 wickets (and one more) for the first time since he had become England captain,

and he had made a fine half-century into the bargain. Botham's entrance did not instantly put an end to England's misfortunes. Yet an off-drive off Alderman, as relaxed as a Taunton afternoon, immediately relieved the walking tragedy of Boycott's departure and the farce of Taylor's dollied catch to Bright at short-leg. Like Gilbert Jessop in 1902, Ian Botham had a point to make, or rather to drive home. And now he was joined by a young man still anxious to establish a place in the England team – Graham Dilley.

Even here, our absentee with half an eye on the TV set could justifiably have decided he was watching nothing more than a last desperate display of fireworks. 'At least they're putting up a fight here,' commented Christopher Martin-Jenkins as Dilley sent the ball crashing through the covers for his highest Test score yet, 39 not out. And a little later, as one of Botham's mighty swings sailed for a boundary he had not necessarily aimed at: 'Not quite what he intended, but it brings up his 80 nevertheless!'

Marsh catches Botham off Lillee to establish a world wicket-keeping record.

Kim Hughes seemed even less aware than the commentators, who should not be too severely censured by those of us with the gift of hindsight and video, of the astonishing change that was creeping over the game. True, the field-placings had been modified from the attacking formations of earlier in the day, which had seen a row of slips watching Botham bombard the boundary area behind the bowler's arm. But the boundary itself remained a picture of unpopulated grass. A ring of fielders now occupied a 'halfway house' between the wicket and the fence, as if ready for the scampered single in the last over of a NatWest final. Botham, of course, had broader objectives.

Writing after the event, Richie Benaud faulted Hughes for failing to bring Alderman round the wicket to fire straight at the left-hander Dilley's stumps. This was not hindsight. 'It was always on the cards,' he commented when Terry Alderman finally came round to send the Kent fast bowler's bails flying, 'once they decided this should be the angle of attack.' Perhaps poor Hughes should have taken the trouble to call at

Richie's commentary box during the tea interval, for when Dilley's wicket fell, 117 runs had been added since the fall of the previous wicket.

Botham and Dilley, like Jessop and Hirst long before them, had discovered the underdog's inherent strength, which is the top dog's blindness to the possibility that he could go under. Botham had his hundred up in 157 minutes, not quite as fast as Jessop's 139 minutes but equally match-swinging in tempo. Besides, Botham would make 44 more runs (and all of them were needed) than Jessop's 104 c Noble b Armstrong. Again, Botham was batting among the tailenders, albeit with unexpected support from Graham Dilley, and now Chris Old.

Meanwhile, back in the pavilion was a man with a deep understanding of psychology and, no doubt, history. It is not unlikely that Mike Brearley remembered how the ancient Greeks had demolished a massively superior Persian fleet at Salamis through the latter's belief that defeat was impossible. In case anyone was beginning to forget that

Ian Botham released from care.

this run-feast was a Test match, he signalled from the balcony that he wished his batsmen to 'stick around' till stumps. This they did, with the last man Willis safely at the bowler's end, where it would be his turn to make history the next day.

Hitherto England had saved Tests with the dead bats of grim defence, as exemplified by Willie Watson and Trevor Bailey in their famous last-ditch stand at Lord's in 1953. But not since The Oval in 1902 had an England team come roaring out of the jaws of defeat to win an impossible victory. 'And yesterday they were burying English cricket!' exulted Christopher Martin-Jenkins as Bob Willis ripped through Australia's second innings. And the miracle was to be repeated at the next Test at Edgbaston.

Cricket, which had been considered 'square' in the 'swinging sixties' and had been soured with controversy in the seventies, now became the 'in' game, in England at least. Every other man, or woman, in the local

Opposite: 'At least they're putting up a fight here!' Graham Dilley lashes out.

ENGLAND *v* AUSTRALIA, 1981

Played at Headingley, 16–21 July
Result: England won by 18 runs

AUSTRALIA

J. Dyson, b Dilley	102	c Taylor, b Willis	34
G.M. Wood, lbw b Botham	34	c Taylor, b Botham	10
T.M. Chappell, c Taylor, b Willey	27	c Taylor, b Willis	8
K.J. Hughes, c and b Botham	89	c Botham, b Willis	0
R.J. Bright, b Dilley	7	G.N. Yallop, c Gatting, b Willis	0
G.N. Yallop, c Taylor, b Botham	58	A.R. Border, b Old	0
A.R. Border, lbw b Botham	8	R.W. Marsh, c Dilley, b Willis	4
R.W. Marsh, b Botham	28	R.J. Bright, b Willis	19
G.F. Lawson, c Taylor, b Botham	13	c Taylor, b Willis	1
D.K. Lillee, not out	3	c Gatting, b Willis	17
		T.M. Alderman, not out	0
B 4, l-b 13, w 3, n-b 12	32	l-b 3, w 1, n-b 14	18
Total (9 wkts dec)	401	Total	111

T.M. Alderman did not bat.

Fall of wickets. First innings: 1–55, 2–149, 3–196, 4–220, 5–332, 6–354, 7–357, 8–396, 9–401. Second innings: 1–13, 2–56, 3–58, 4–58, 5–65, 6–68, 7–74, 8–75, 9–110, 10–111.

ENGLAND

G.A. Gooch, lbw b Alderman	2	c Alderman, b Lillee	0
G. Boycott, b Lawson	12	lbw b Alderman	46
J.M. Brearley, c Marsh, b Alderman	10	c Alderman, b Lillee	14
D.I. Gower, c Marsh, b Lawson	24	c Border, b Alderman	9
M.W. Gatting, lbw b Lillee	15	lbw b Alderman	1
P. Willey, b Lawson	8	c Dyson, b Lillee	33
I.T. Botham, c Marsh, b Lillee	50	not out	149
R.W. Taylor, c Marsh, b Lillee	5	c Bright, b Alderman	1
G.R. Dilley, c and b Lillee	13	b Alderman	58
C.M. Old, c Border, b Alderman	0	b Lawson	29
R.G.D. Willis, not out	1	c Border, b Alderman	2
B 6, l-b 11, w 6, n-b 11	34	B 5, l-b 3, w 3, n-b 5	16
Total	174	Total	358

Fall of wickets. First innings: 1–12, 2–40, 3–42, 4–84, 5–87, 6–112, 7–148, 8–166, 9–167, 10–174. Second innings: 1–0, 2–18, 3–37, 4–41, 5–105, 6–133, 7–135, 8–252, 9–319, 10–358.

BOWLING ANALYSIS

ENGLAND

	O	M	R	W		O	M	R	W
Willis	30	8	72	0	Willis	15.1	3	43	8
Old	43	14	91	0	Old	9	1	21	1
Dilley	27	4	78	2	Dilley	2	0	11	0
Botham	38.2	11	95	6	Botham	7	3	14	1
Willey	13	2	31	1	Willey	3	1	4	0
Boycott	3	2	2	0					

AUSTRALIA

	O	M	R	W		O	M	R	W
Lillee	18.5	7	49	4	Lillee	25	6	94	3
Alderman	19	4	59	3	Alderman	35.3	0	135	6
Lawson	13	3	32	3	Lawson	23	4	96	1
					Bright	4	0	15	0

England followed on.

Umpires: B.J. Meyer and D.G. Evans

or the club became a cricket 'nut'. Sponsorship and corporate participation in the game increased from this date and, incidentally, cricket literature flourished. Possibly, too, people with tickets for the Monday of a Test now made sure they were in their seats by lunch-time – at least if Botham was still batting.

WARWICKSHIRE v HAMPSHIRE, 1922

The Oval 1902 and Headingley 1981 Tests represent breathtaking reversals of fortune; but in terms of statistics, at least, it is doubtful whether any tale of the unexpected can rival Warwickshire v Hampshire, played at Edgbaston, 14–16 June 1922. Why the Hon. L.H. Tennyson of Hampshire decided, after winning the toss, to invite his fellow 'Hon.', the Hon. F.S.G. Calthorpe of Warwickshire, to bat has never been satisfactorily explained. 'You're asking us to bat first on this billiard table?' Calthorpe exclaimed in disbelief.

Warwickshire may have been slightly disappointed to make only 223 on such a surface, until they dismissed Hampshire for 15 runs! Eight batsmen failed to score – a Hants record in itself – in what was by far the lowest total ever recorded by the county. Understandably, Calthorpe invited Hampshire to follow on. Besides, the founder of the Cricket Golf Society had plans for a day off on the fairways. In the event, he was detained in the field the whole of the next day and into the following morning as Hampshire compiled 521 runs.

Lionel Tennyson started things rolling with a 'light brigade' charge which produced 45 runs in an hour. Then, Hampshire's great all-rounder George Brown tore into Warwickshire's bowlers like a Botham – he scored 172. Meanwhile, wicket-keeper Livesey, batting at number ten, did a Walter Read, scoring 110 not out. Incredibly for anyone who had watched Hampshire's first-innings efforts, Warwickshire now required 312 runs to win. They made only 158 of them. There never was a more striking advertisement for the unpredictability of cricket.

FOWLER'S MATCH, JULY 1910

'The roars from the Harrow Stand whenever a run was scored were heard in the Zoological Gardens,' wrote a spectator of the Eton v Harrow match at Lord's in 1910. The excitement generated by what, when all is said and done, was a match between two teams of schoolboys, was to reach beyond the Regent's Park Zoo to the highest echelons of government. At the game's end, 'one of the most eminent of our statesmen was seen dancing on some dark blue emblem with tears coursing down his cheeks', wrote another spectator, the Hon. Edward Lyttelton.

In 1910, Eton v Harrow was an important fixture. Cricket apart, it represented one of the most glittering events of the London social season. During the lunch and tea intervals, the rich, the powerful and the beautiful strolled across the field of play in a fashion parade at least as impressive as Royal Ascot. But interest in the game was not confined to old school enthusiasts and boys wearing stiff collars or straw hats. At a time when Test series were relatively few and far between and one-day finals were unheard of, such an occasion ranked with Oxford v Cambridge and Gentlemen v Players as one of the season's high spots.

Nothing happened during the first morning, a Friday, to disturb the traditional social pleasantries, apart from one or two unwelcome showers. Harrow made 232 at a steady pace as dowagers cruised the boundary in search of eligible young bachelors to introduce to their débutante daughters and nieces. Then drama began to intrude on the social intercourse. Eton were rushed out for 67. Only one batsman managed to reach double figures. Eton's captain, R.StL. Fowler, who

WARWICKSHIRE v HAMPSHIRE, 1922

Played at Edgbaston, 14–16 June
Result: Hampshire won by 155 runs

WARWICKSHIRE

Bates, c Shirley, b Newman....	3	c Mead, b Kennedy.........	1
Smith, c Mead, b Newman....	24	c Shirley, b Kennedy........	41
F.R. Santall, c McIntyre, b Boyes	84	b Newman................	0
W.G. Quaife, b Newman......	1	not out	40
Hon. F.S.G. Calthorpe, c Boyes, b Kennedy	70	b Newman................	30
Rev. E.F. Waddy, c Mead, b Boyes	0	b Newman................	0
B.W. Quaife, b Boyes........	0	c and b Kennedy	7
Fox, b Kennedy...........	4	b Kennedy...............	0
J. Smart, b Newman.........	20	b Newman...............	3
C. Smart, c Mead, b Boyes	14	c and b Boyes............	15
H. Howell, not out.........	1	c Kennedy, b Newman.......	11
Extras................	2	Extras................	10
Total	223	Total	158

HAMPSHIRE

Bowell, b Howell	0	c Howell, b Quaife (W.G.)	45
Kennedy, c Smith, b Calthorpe .	0	b Calthorpe	7
H.L.V. Day, b Calthorpe	0	c Bates, b Quaife (W.G.)......	15
Mead, not out	6	b Howell	24
Hon. L.H. Tennyson, c Calthorpe, b Howell	4	c Smart (C.), b Calthorpe	45
Brown, b Howell	0	b Smart (C.)	172
Newman, c Smart (C.), b Howell	0	c and b Quaife (W.G.)	12
W.R. Shirley, c Smart (J.), b Calthorpe	1	lbw, b Fox...............	30
A.S. McIntyre, lbw, b Calthorpe	0	lbw, b Howell	5
Livsey, b Howell	0	not out	110
Boyes, lbw, b Howell	0	b Howell	29
Extras................	4	Extras................	27
Total	15	Total	521

BOWLING ANALYSIS

HAMPSHIRE

	O	M	R	W		O	M	R	W
Kennedy.........	24	7	74	2	Kennedy.........	26	12	47	4
Newman.........	12.3	0	70	4	Newman.........	26.3	12	53	5
Boyes...........	16	5	56	4	Boyes...........	11	4	34	1
Shirley.........	3	0	21	0	Brown	5	0	14	0

WARWICKSHIRE

	O	M	R	W		O	M	R	W
Howell..........	4.5	2	7	6	Howell..........	63	10	156	3
Calthorpe........	4	3	4	4	Calthorpe........	33	7	97	2
					Quaife (W.G.).....	49	8	154	3
					Fox	7	0	30	1
					Smart (J.)........	13	2	37	0
					Santall	5	0	15	0
					Smart (C.)	1	0	5	1

Umpires: Atfield and B. Brown.

was destined to give his name to the match, achieved top score with 21.

Harrow's captain Guy Earle, later to do great things for Somerset, may have hesitated before enforcing the follow-on for fear of upsetting the sociabilities of the Saturday. In the event, he opted for ruthlessness. Eton batted again and were soon 2 wickets down for 19, Tufnell's wicket being captured by a young left-arm spinner who featured on the scorecard as R.H.L.G. Alexander. (This bowler was later to capture the more important 'wicket' of Rome as Field-Marshal Lord Alexander of

Opposite: Social comment takes precedence in these sketches of the match.

Tunis.) Many Old Etonians now left the ground in disgust, deserting what they confidently believed was a sinking ship. The rain that fell that night must have represented the only hope for the Eton supporters that the old school would escape with a draw.

A sparser crowd watched things go from bad to worse for Eton the following morning, 'doubtless owing to the fact that there was a strong impression the match would come to an early termination', commented *The Observer*. A majority of Harrow rosette-wearers saw Eton lose 5 wickets for 65. The dowagers still remaining on the ground hurried to complete their introductions. After all, Eton were still 104 runs short of avoiding defeat by an innings.

Only Robert Fowler refused to budge. Indeed, he weighed into the Harrow bowling to score a brilliant 64, the highest innings of the match as it happened. At least he had helped to make certain that Harrow would have to bat again. Yet when the last pair came together, there was a credit balance of only 4 runs.

John Manners was an affable young man who had been picked solely for his fielding. As a batsman, he was the owner of 'the crookedest bat ever seen at Lord's'. Nevertheless, he now commenced to clout the ball to all corners of the field. His very unorthodoxy helped his cause to prosper. 'Not only was it impossible to anticipate where he would hit next,' wrote Lyttelton, 'watching him as I did from the Grand Stand through an opera glass, I could not tell from the swing of the bat where to look for the ball.' No more could Harrow's fielders. Manners was supported first by Lister-Kaye and then by eleventh man W.G.K. Boswell, presumably in the side for his occasional bowling. He now contributed 32 runs in a famous last stand that brought Eton to the respectable total of 219.

There is a poignant story attaching to John Manners' extraordinary innings. His father, Lord Manners, had left the ground in despair at Eton's poor showing at lunch-time and locked himself in his study with orders that he was on no account to be disturbed. A butler rapped unavailingly at his door with the information that his son had saved Eton from an innings defeat – indeed, that he had put Harrow to the trouble of having to score 54 runs for victory. The feelings of Lord Manners when he finally emerged from his study must have been grievous. (His son, incidentally, was to die on the Western Front in 1914.)

As was the case with the two Test matches we have described in this section, a sensational batting recovery was accomplished on an uneasy surface, for the sun returned to Lord's on Saturday 9 July 1910 to put a touch of devilry into the soaked turf. 'Look here,' said the Eton cricket master back in the dressing room, 'if you fellows field up there is no reason why you should not win the match.' This wildly optimistic thought was echoed by A.G. Steel, Eton's greatest cricketer. He added meaningfully, 'It was on just such a wicket as this that I bowled out seven of the Players in 1883 for 43 runs.'

In the meantime, a posse of Old Harrovian authorities had gathered around the wicket in order to decide what roller to use. In their combined wisdom they opted for the heaviest roller available, with the aim of drawing moisture and 'devil' out of the wicket. It was a momentous miscalculation. All the wicket's awkwardness was compacted under a thin, dry surface that gave every possible encouragement to the fast off-break, which happened to be R.StL. Fowler's stock in trade. With his first ball he sent Wilson of Harrow's bails flying. Then he bowled Jameson for 2 with a prodigious break back.

It was at this point that animals in Regent's Park Zoo were disturbed from their slumbers, and the mad dash for Lord's began. One Old Etonian, Lieutenant-Colonel C.P. Foley, sprang from a barber's chair and jumped into a taxi, issuing a command which has echoed down the

THE MOST SENSATIONAL ETON AND HARROW MATCH.

DRAWN BY FRANK REYNOLDS.

SPECTATORS AND ACTORS IN THE EXTRAORDINARY CONTEST BETWEEN ETON AND HARROW, JULY 8 AND 9, 1910:
SKETCHES AT LORD'S.

Opposite: The 'hoisting' of Fowler. Eton colours fly from a forest of umbrellas.

ETON v HARROW, 1910

Played at Lord's, 8–9 July
Result: Eton won by 9 runs

HARROW

T.O. Jameson, c Lubbock, b Fowler	5	b Fowler	2
T.B. Wilson, b Kaye	53	b Fowler	0
G.W.V. Hopley, b Fowler	35	b Fowler	8
T.L.G. Turnbull, lbw b Fowler	2	c Boswell, b Fowler	0
G.F. Earle (capt), c Wigan, b Steel	20	c Wigan, b Fowler	13
W.T. Monckton,[1] c Lubbock, b Stock	20	b Fowler	0
J.M. Hillyard, st Lubbock, b Fowler	62	c Kaye, b Fowler	0
C.H.B. Blount, c Holland, b Steel	4	c and b Steel	5
A.C. Straker, c Holland, b Steel	2	b Fowler	1
O.B. Graham, c and b Steel	6	not out	7
Hon. R.H.L.G. Alexander,[1] not out	2	c Holland, b Steel	8
B 18, l-b 2, n-b 1	21	B 1	1
Total	232	Total	45

ETON

R.H. Lubbock, lbw b Earle	9	c Straker, b Hillyard	9
C.W. Tufnell, b Hillyard	5	lbw, b Alexander	7
W.T. Birchenough, c Hopley, b Graham	5	c Turnbull, b Jameson	22
W.T. Holland, c Hopley, b Hillyard	2	st Monckton, b Alexander	5
R.stL. Fowler (capt), c Graham, b Jameson	21	c Earle, b Hillyard	64
A.I. Steel,[1] b Graham	0	c Hopley, b Hillyard	6
D.G. Wigan, c Turnbull, b Jameson	8	b Graham	16
A.B. Stock, lbw b Alexander	2	lbw, b Earle	0
Hon J.N. Manners, c Graham, b Alexander	4	not out	40
K. Lister Kaye, c Straker, b Alexander	0	c Jameson, b Earle	13
W.G.K. Boswell, not out	0	b Earle	32
B 10, w 1	11	B 2, w 3	5
Total	67	Total	219

[1]The Hon. R.H.L.G. Alexander later became the famous Field-Marshal, and W.T. Monckton was later Sir Walter Monckton KC. A.I. Steel was a son of A.G. Steel.

BOWLING ANALYSIS

ETON

	O	M	R	W		O	M	R	W
Fowler	37.3	9	90	4	Fowler	10	2	23	8
Steel	31	11	69	4	Steel	6.4	1	12	2
Kaye	12	5	23	1	Kaye	3	0	9	0
Stock	7	2	12	1					
Boswell	8	4	17	0					

HARROW

	O	M	R	W		O	M	R	W
Earle	12	9	4	1	Earle	17.3	3	57	3
Hillyard	19	9	38	2	Hillyard	23	7	65	3
Graham	9	7	3	2	Graham	8	12	33	1
Jameson	4	1	4	2	Jameson	9	1	26	1
Alexander	4.1	1	7	3	Alexander	14	4	33	2
					Wilson	2	2	0	0

Umpires: J. Moss and J.P. Whiteside

THE ETON CAPTAIN NEARLY TORN TO PIECES BY HIS ADMIRERS.

DRAWN BY S. BEGG.

THE HERO OF THE MATCH: MR. R. ST. L. FOWLER INTERCEPTED BY HIS FELLOW-ETONIANS AT LORD'S.

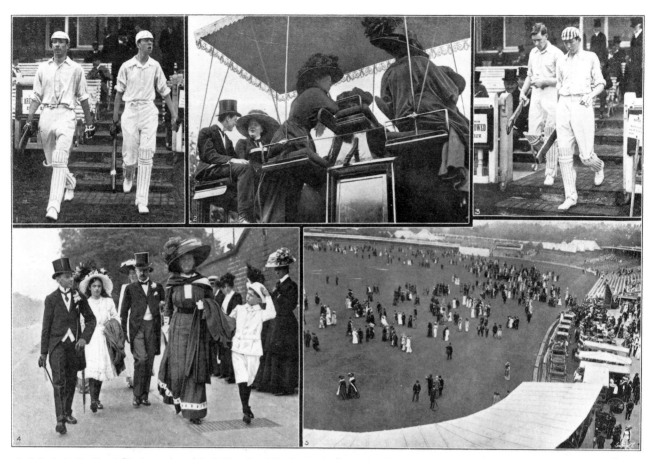

1. *R. St. L. Fowler (21 and 64), the captain, and D. G. Wigan (8 and 16) off to bat for Eton on Saturday morning.* 2. *From the coach tops.* 3. *T. O. Jameson (5 and 2) and T. B. Wilson (53 and 0) off to start Harrow's fatal last innings.* 4. *Arrivals.* 5. *During the luncheon interval.*

ETON v. HARROW AT LORD'S.—A NINE RUNS VICTORY FOR THE ETONIANS.

Pictured among the dowagers, Eton's and Harrow's opening pairs.

years: 'Lord's, driver! Double fare if you do it in fifteen minutes!'

Guy Earle held on grimly for 13; but all around him wickets were crashing to Fowler. Among the victims was a future cabinet minister, Sir Walter Monckton. Score: 0. In a career which was to find him involved in many top-level crises, including the Abdication, Monckton never forgot his failure to rise to this occasion. 'It's a horrible reflection,' he confessed to his biographer, 'that at the most critical moment Bob Fowler bowled me with a slow full-pitch.'

Another future cabinet minister and commander, Field-Marshal Lord Alexander of Tunis, showed, in contrast, that he had no intention of surrender. In his last-wicket stand with O.B. Graham, he suggested how effortless a victory for Harrow could still be. Then A.G. Steel's son found the edge of Alexander's bat. Holland in the slips held the ball on high. Eton had won by 9 runs; and Eton supporters went totally mad. A.J. Balfour did a dance on the pavilion steps. Colonel Foley, he of the half-completed haircut, bayonetted an Old Harrovian with his umbrella. Politicians, colonial governors and magistrates ran like schoolboys on to the field to 'hoist' Fowler, who must have been grateful of the ride for he had scarcely been off the field the entire match.

Now the news started to spread. 'Far down Baker Street and even near to Grosvenor Square, O.E.s who had stayed to the end shouted from taxi and bus the incredible news,' wrote Lyttelton. The West End had not seen anything like the night of 'Fowler's Match' since Mafeking's relief, and yet this victory had nothing to do with war; it was only a cricket match between schoolboys. Here again was proof, perhaps the most conclusive so far, of cricket's power to engage the most profound emotions, including, in this case, those of the highest in the land.

3
ENDINGS
AND BEGINNINGS

It's time to focus on a number of matches which, while they may not have given much pleasure to their spectators, could be said to have brought the curtain down on an era and thereby heralded new approaches and methods.

AMERICA'S COLD SHOULDER

An Eleven of England *v* Twenty-two of the United States and Canada in 1859 was by no means the last attempt to convert America to cricket. Other tours were to follow, and W.G. Grace, Richard Daft and Ranji would feature among them. In addition, as we have seen, cricket was to flourish for a while in Philadelphia. Yet this 1859 match seems to symbolize the essential failure of the mission.

It must be admitted that 24 October is not the ideal time of year to embark on a cricket match, least of all at Rochester in upper New York state. Yet this was the time and the place of a notable meeting between Frederick Lillywhite's English tourists and the massed strength of the United States and Canada.

As can be seen from the scorecard, the North Americans made heavy weather of the Englishmen's attack; but the climate was even crueller on

The voyage out. Lillywhite's team *en route* for America.

145

ELEVEN OF ENGLAND *v* TWENTY-TWO OF THE STATES AND CANADA 1859

Played at Rochester, USA, 21, 24 and 25 October
Result: England won by an innings and 70 runs

TWENTY-TWO

W. Hammond, c Carpenter, b Wisden	4	b Wisden	6
Sharp, st Lockyer, b Wisden	0	b Jackson	4
D.S. Booth, b Wisden	1	st Lockyer, b Jackson	0
Beatty, st Lockyer, b Wisden	2	b Wisden	0
H. Wright, b Jackson	13	b Jackson	1
Capt Hammond, run out	2	c and b Wisden	0
Capt K. Hugesson, b Wisden	2	b Jackson	3
Machattie, c and b Wisden	0	st Lockyer, b Wisden	1
Pickering, run out	11	not out	14
Stephenson, b Wisden	0	absent	0
J. Higham, st Lockyer, b Wisden	0	c Carpenter, b Jackson	0
T. Senior, b Jackson	1	b Wisden	8
A. Jackson, b Wisden	0	st Lockyer, b Wisden	0
Collis, b Jackson	0	st Lockyer, b Wisden	4
Tarrant, b Wisden	0	b Wisden	2
Crossley, not out	3	c Carpenter, b Wisden	0
Hines, b Wisden	0	b Wisden	4
G. Tarrant, b Wisden	0	b Jackson	2
H. Lillywhite, c Carpenter, b Wisden	0	b Wisden	0
Wm. Collis, b Wisden	0	absent	0
Hallis, c Lockyer, b Wisden	0	c Carpenter, b Wisden	9
Pattison, c Caesar, b Wisden	0	c Jackson, b Wisden	0
		B 1, l-b 2, w 1	4
Total	**39**	**Total**	**62**

ENGLAND

W. Caffyn, c Hammond, b Hallis	14
J. Jackson, run out	12
T. Hayward, c Hallis, b Crossley	50
R. Carpenter, c Hines, b Senior	18
J. Grundy, c Higham, b Pickering	8
T. Lockyer, c Hallis, b Wright	19
A. Diver, c Hines, b Machattie	6
John Lillywhite, b Wright	4
J. Caesar, st Higham, b Machattie	11
J. Wisden, c Lillywhite, b Machattie	2
H.H. Stephenson, not out	1
B 6, w 20	26
Total	**171**

BOWLING ANALYSIS

ENGLAND

	O	M	R	W		O	M	R	W
Wisden	72	7	17	16	Wisden	89	4	43	13
Jackson	68	7	17	3	Jackson	84	13	17	6

TWENTY-TWO

	O	M	R	W
Hallis	136	12	46	1
Sharp	8	0	16	0
Senior	68	8	17	1
Crossley	20	4	2	0
Pickering	48	3	21	1
H. Wright	48	2	35	3
Machattie	36	4	8	3

Umpires: W. Baker of Ottawa and Smith of Utica

the fielders. 'The players had to field in muffs and greatcoats,' reported Frederick Lillywhite, 'and such was the cold they scarcely knew whether they had fielded the ball or not.' Naturally, the conditions were equally adverse for the batsmen. 'Shiver my timbers, I'm out!' cried one North American batsman with undisguised relief when John Wisden demolished his wicket.

The match was to have been a three-day affair. In the event, no play was possible on the second day and on the third the match ended early with a victory for the visiting Englishmen by an innings and 70 runs. Here we come to the most disappointing outcome of the 'Frosty Match', as it was forever to be remembered by the English participants. The promoters, in a desperate effort to recoup their investment, organized an impromptu baseball match. The expansion of cricket had been frozen in its tracks; the alternative entertainment was to prove a hardier survivor in this corner of the world.

Frederick Lillywhite's 'England' tourists in America, 1859. The tour ended with a baseball match.

TEN DAYS THAT CHANGED THE TEST WORLD

Warwick Armstrong read a newspaper in the field at The Oval in 1921 in protest against time limits in Tests. He argued, as did many Australian authorities, that a true Test needed to be played to a finish. This, indeed, was how Tests were played down under until 1946/7.

England's administrators tended to take an opposite point of view. In deference to the demands of brighter cricket and the county programme, they allotted only three days to Tests in the period 1900 to 1926. In 1930 a fourth day was added, but not until 1948 was the first five-day Test played in England. Only if the series was undecided when the teams came to the Fifth Test were the administrators prepared to bend to Australian pressure. In 1934 and 1938 the Fifth Oval Tests were designated as 'timeless', although four days proved sufficient in

Walter Hammond (right) and Bill Edrich (above), century and double-century makers in a ten-day marathon.

both cases. It would have been otherwise in 1938 if Bradman had not had to retire injured.

Even so, the 'timeless' Test at The Oval in 1938 contained ingredients which an English public was to find attractive. After all the hammerings they had suffered from Bradman, it was an agreeable experience to watch, or listen on the wireless, as England with all the time in the world piled up the record total of 903 which included, of course, Hutton's Bradman-beating 364. Besides, this was the 1930s, the period of marathon-singing contests and four- to five-day 'dancethons'.

In any case, there seemed to be a future for timelessness in Tests until England met South Africa in the Fifth Test at Durban for virtually the first half of March, in 1939. A series between two immensely strong batting sides, both weaker in bowling, had seen three draws and one

victory for England. It was decided that the final Test should last as long as it took to enable South Africa either to square the series or to confirm England in her ascendancy. Here is a brief day-by-day summary of the action, or the inaction as the case may be.

First day
South Africa won the toss and decided to bat. 49 for 2 wickets at lunch, they finished at 229 for 2. Van der Byl 105 not out.
Second day
South Africa added 194 runs to the total, ending the day at 423 for 6. Van der Byl 125 (b Perks) in 7 hours 18 minutes.
Third day
South Africa all out for 530 in 13 hours. A.D. Nourse 103 (b Perks). In 45 minutes L. Hutton and P.A. Gibb scored 10 runs.

Fourth day
England 268 for 6.
Fifth day
England all out for 316. South Africa second innings 193 for 3.
Sixth day
South Africa all out for 481. A. Melville (b Farnes) 103. England are set 696 to win.
Seventh day
England 253 for 1. P.A. Gibb 107 not out.
Eighth day
No play owing to rain.
Ninth day
England 496 for 3. P.A. Gibb (b Dalton) 120. W.J. Edrich (c Gordon, b Langton) 219.
Tenth day
England 654 for 5. W.R. Hammond (st Grieveson, b Dalton) 140. Rain stops play.

In fact, it will be seen that the scoring rate was not significantly lower than that achieved in the England *v* New Zealand Tests in New Zealand in March 1988, though the innings totals in the former case are considerably higher than the average for the more recent series. On the eleventh or, conceivably, the twelfth day the Durban match could have come to a grandstand finish. However, it was now recalled that the England team had a booking on the *Athlone Castle*, which was shortly due to sail for home. After ten days of toil, this extraordinary Test match was abandoned as a draw. The experiment was not repeated. Although the length of Test matches has varied, a time limit is now the norm throughout the Test playing world.

DEAD END FOR THE DEAD BAT

Opposite and above: Two lively moments in a dreary Test series. Tony Lock is the bowler in both pictures. Neil Harvey is his victim in the second.

Test 'crawls' have by no means been confined to timeless matches. In the late 1950s, slow scoring threatened to destroy the market for Test cricket. Some of the responsibility for this trend has to be laid at the door of Sir Leonard Hutton. Under intense pressure to achieve favourable results for England, Hutton would, if the need arose, resort to delaying tactics with the bat and the over rates. We have already mentioned Watson's and Bailey's great defensive stand in the Lord's Test against Australia in 1953 where a patriotic crowd had watched enraptured as Willie Watson (109 runs in 5 hours 50 minutes) and Trevor Bailey (71 in 4 and a half hours) had denied Hassett's men what had seemed a certain victory. The Watson–Bailey stand enabled England to go on to win back the Ashes; but it may also have helped to create false conceptions both of what was acceptable in terms of Test entertainment and of what was expedient in terms of cricket strategy.

When England visited Australia in 1958–9, Peter May (the present Chairman of Selectors) had succeeded Hutton as England captain. May was a delightful, natural player, but as a captain he took the 'safety first' policy to lengths which were to lead to disaster.

The First Test match, played at Brisbane in December 1958, was unique in that the majority of English journalists following the tour were actually pleased that Australia won. The wicket was lively, yet England's first-day score of 134 all out, occupying all but two overs of play, is indicative of the attitude that was adopted towards the challenge. Loader, Bailey and Laker did well to restrict Australia to 186 in her first innings. They also achieved a psychological success in temporarily persuading the Australians that go-slow batting was the key to achievement. Australia's bright new batting star, Norman O'Neill, took two and a half hours to score 34.

Now Peter May raised the stakes in defensiveness. He promoted 'Barnacle' Bailey to number three with orders to stay put until the spinners, Laker and Lock, could bowl on a worn wicket. In mitigation

Richie Benaud. With Frank
Worrell he engineered bright
approaches to Tests.

Opposite: Sir Garfield Sobers –
delighted the Brisbane crowd
with a brilliant century.

of Bailey's efforts it must be said that the Australian bowling was hostile and wickets were falling steadily. Nevertheless, the paying public was now treated to the spectacle of England scoring 198 in eight and a half hours, to which Trevor Bailey contributed 68 in 458 minutes.

It was, however, a useless effort. The fifth-day wicket played relatively easily. Norman O'Neill departed from all previous form shown in this match, including his own, to score a thrilling 71 in 115 minutes. Wrote E.M. Wellings, who was reporting the series for the *Evening News*:

> This was a game that miserably distorted cricket and happily for the game's future was punished by defeat . . . a beautiful innings by Norman O'Neill not only won the match but in the most striking manner pointed out the error of the English batting ways.

A TALE OF TWO BRISBANES

In its perverse way, this gruesome match saved Test cricket in Australia. We have already seen how Sir Donald Bradman moved to curb the abuses of chucking and dragging that had further marred the 1958/9 series. Similarly, he determined to put an end to pointless, time-wasting tedium. Two years later, in 1960, the West Indies visited Australia. Both captains, Richie Benaud of Australia and Frank Worrell of West Indies, were enjoined to provide entertainment first and foremost. In fact, the two men needed little encouragement.

The First Test at Brisbane was played as if every man on the field and in the committee room was determined to banish the spectre of the notorious 'Battle of the Snooze'. The Brisbane crowd was astonished to see Conrad Hunte of West Indies off-drive the third ball of the match for four and, without drawing breath, hook the next for a boundary to leg. A brilliant century by Gary Sobers and an elegant 65 by Worrell were among the entertainments on view in a day which saw the 200 up at five minutes past two and a close-of-play total of 359 for 7 on the board. Jack Fingleton was not the only correspondent to point out the comparison with a total of 142 runs scored on the corresponding day in the Test with England two years earlier.

The crowd, now around 16,000, was being spoiled with stroke-play; so much so that when Norman O'Neill and 'Slasher' Mackay toiled in their efforts to overhaul West Indies' 453 total, they were booed by their compatriots. In fact, O'Neill and Co. were laying the foundations for the most thrilling finish in Test history. Australia reached 505 – a first-innings lead of 52. West Indies battled to 284 in their second innings. On the final day, Australia were set 233 to win.

Throughout Australia's innings, the pendulum swung like a grandfather clock gone crazy. First, that great fast bowler Wes Hall had 2 wickets down for 7 – the valuable ones of Neil Harvey and Bobby Simpson. Colin McDonald and Norman O'Neill steadied things for a while. Then Wes Hall struck again. Five wickets were down for 92. Now came solid resistance from Mackay, Benaud and, above all, from Alan Davidson, run out for 80. The pace was becoming frantic.

Batsmen numbers nine and ten were now together and 3 runs were needed for an Australian win. Batsman number ten, Ian Meckiff, swung manfully at an express delivery from Wes Hall. The ball seemed to fly to the boundary, to the accompaniment of delirious cheers. But the groundsman, bewitched perhaps by whatever power was working for an unforgettable finish, had left the grass uncut on this frontier. Conrad Hunte clawed the ball back from the whitewash line and threw straight and fast to the keeper as the batsmen crossed for the third run. Batsman nine, Wally Grout, was run out in a cloud of dust.

Now the scores were level. With the last pair together, Australia

AUSTRALIA *v* WEST INDIES, 1960

First Test match, played at Brisbane, 9, 10, 12, 13 and 14 December
Result: the match was tied

WEST INDIES

C. Hunte, c Benaud, b Davidson	24	c Simpson, b Mackay	39
C. Smith, c Grout, b Davidson .	7	c O'Neill, b Davidson	6
R. Kanhai, c Grout, b Davidson	15	c Grout, b Davidson	54
G. Sobers, c Kline, b Meckiff . .	132	b Davidson	14
F. Worrell, c Grout, b Davidson	65	c Grout, b Davidson	65
J. Solomon, hit wkt, b Simpson .	65	lbw b Simpson	47
P. Lashley, c Grout, b Kline . . .	19	b Davidson	0
G. Alexander, c Davidson, b Kline	60	b Benaud	5
S. Ramadhin, c Harvey, b Davidson	12	c Harvey, b Simpson	6
W. Hall, st Grout, b Kline	50	b Davidson	18
A. Valentine, not out	0	not out	7
l-b 2, w 1	4	B 14, l-b 7, w 2	23
Total	**453**	**Total**	**284**

Fall of wickets. First innings: 1–23, 2–42, 3–65, 4–239, 5–243, 6–283, 7–347, 8–366, 9–452, 10–453. Second innings: 1–13, 2–88, 3–114, 4–127, 5–210, 6–210, 7–241, 8–250, 9–253, 10–284.

AUSTRALIA

C. McDonald, c Hunte, b Sobers	57	b Worrell	16
R. Simpson, b Ramadhin	92	c sub, b Hall	0
N. Harvey, b Valentine	15	c Sobers, b Hall	5
N. O'Neill, c Valentine, b Hall	181	c Alexander, b Hall	26
L. Favell, run out	45	c Solomon, b Hall	7
K. Mackay, b Sobers	35	b Ramadhin	28
A. Davidson, c Alexander, b Hall	44	run out	80
R. Benaud, lbw b Hall	10	c Alexander, b Hall	52
W. Grout, lbw b Hall	4	run out	2
I. Meckiff, run out	4	run out	2
L. Kline, not out	3	not out	0
B 2, l-b 8, w 1, n-b 4	15	B 2, l-b 9, n-b 3	14
Total	**505**	**Total**	**232**

Fall of wickets. First innings: 1–84, 2–138, 3–194, 4–278, 5–381, 6–469, 7–484, 8–489, 9–496, 10–505. Second innings: 1–1, 2–7, 3–49, 4–49, 5–57, 6–92, 7–226, 8–228, 9–232, 10–232.

BOWLING ANALYSIS

AUSTRALIA

	O	M	R	W		O	M	R	W
Davidson	30	2	135	5	Davidson	24.6	4	87	6
Meckiff	18	0	129	1	Meckiff	4	1	19	0
Mackay	3	0	15	0	Mackay	21	7	52	1
Benaud	24	3	93	0	Benaud	31	6	69	1
Simpson	8	0	25	1	Simpson	7	2	18	2
Kline	17.6	6	52	3	Kline	4	0	14	0
					O'Neill	1	0	2	0

WEST INDIES

	O	M	R	W		O	M	R	W
Hall	29.3	1	140	4	Hall	17.7	3	63	5
Worrell	30	0	93	0	Worrell	16	3	41	1
Sobers	32	0	115	2	Sobers	8	0	30	0
Valentine	24	6	82	1	Valentine	10	4	27	0
Ramadhin	15	1	60	1	Ramadhin	17	3	57	1

needed only 1 run to win. As a final twist to a moment of supreme suspense, only two balls remained to be bowled in the match. Last man Lindsay Kline hoiked the last ball but one round to leg and set off like a rabbit. Joe Solomon picked up and threw in one spontaneous movement. From his angle only one stump was in vision. He scored a direct hit as Meckiff's bat lunged for the crease.

It so happened that Australia's top cricket broadcasters, anticipating a draw, had flown back to Sydney earlier in the afternoon, leaving a cub reporter to mind the mike. His voice can still be heard on tape exultantly acclaiming what he believed was an Australian win. Of course, the real result was an astonishing tie – the first ever recorded in Tests.

The 'Tied Test' at Brisbane brought Test cricket bouncing out of the sickroom, where many had begun to despair for its life. But would the recovery have been quite so startling if the events at Brisbane two years earlier had not forced the authorities to apply radical remedies?

It's a tie! Yet an Australian commentator hailed the result as a victory for Australia.

THE OVER THAT ENDED THROWING

Earlier in the year at Lord's, in a fittingly sombre contest, another disturbing tendency was stopped dead in its tracks: throwing.

For the 1960 tour of England, the South African selectors had included a young pace bowler of emphatically suspect action, Geoff Griffin, in the party. Perhaps they had seen a green light in the failure of the Australian umpires to 'call' Meckiff and Rorke in the 1958/9 Tests. Or possibly they recalled the discreet intervention of Sir Pelham

The humiliation of Geoff Griffin. The South African bowler is obliged to complete his over underarm. Umpire Buller watches from square leg.

Warner on behalf of Cuan McCarthy during their 1951 tour. In the summer of 1960, however, Pelham Warner was ailing and there were to be no gentle whispers in umpires' ears. Griffin, the pleasantest of fast men, was left to take his chance on the open market. Until the Second Test at Lord's he enjoyed the benefit of a certain amount of doubt, though he was 'called' in the matches against MCC, Nottinghamshire and Hampshire.

Now he was to experience, in a single Test match, both the pinnacle of achievement and the depths of rejection and, no doubt, personal despair. With the wickets of Mike Smith, Peter Walker and Ray Illingworth he became the first South African to bring off the hat-trick in Tests. Yet the applause had hardly died down before he was no-balled by umpire Frank Lee at square leg. In fact, Griffin was no-balled eleven times by Lee during England's first innings of 362 for 8 wickets. Since Griffin had sent down 30 overs and taken 4 wickets, Griffin and his captain, Jackie McGlew, may have reckoned that this was a just acceptable rate of wastage. Meanwhile, South Africa were shot out by Statham, Moss and Trueman for 152 and 137. From Griffin's point of view, the match ended too early.

An exhibition game was arranged, and the umpires changed ends. Now Griffin was bowling with England's senior umpire, Sid Buller, at square leg. It was the first time in the tour that the two men had been so positioned. Buller seems to have decided that since Griffin's arm was fundamentally bent, there was no point in selective calling. He no-balled Griffin's first four deliveries. Skipper McGlew was bound to intervene. He advised Griffin to complete his over underarm. Now a double humiliation was heaped on poor Griffin: as he began his first 'back-garden' delivery he was immediately no-balled by umpire Lee, perhaps somewhat churlishly, for failing to give notice of a change of action.

In later life, Sid Buller was to be haunted by the 'Griffin affair' and the personal tragedy he had been instrumental in bringing about. Yet with those four consecutive shouts of 'no ball!', Buller saved cricket from a development that could have changed the game beyond all recognition.

4
THE ONE-DAY REVOLUTION

It could be claimed that the most significant cricket match in the last twenty-five years was that played between Kent and Sussex at Tunbridge Wells on 22 May 1963. No other days were scheduled for this contest, for it was among the first one-day limited-over games ever played.

Sixteen counties met each other on this 1963 May day in the first round of the new Gillette Cup competition. We single out the match at Tunbridge Wells because, before the new form of cricket was a day old, Sussex had demonstrated the spectacular acceleration in scoring it could produce. Sussex had 314 for 7 on the board by mid afternoon, a good score on any full day of a normal county match, and Ken Suttle had run up one of the competition's first centuries; as many as four were scored on that notable day! Sussex beat Kent by 72 runs, but more important than the result was the fact that 556 runs had been scored in a single day. Richie Benaud, who was present at Tunbridge Wells, was asked if he was surprised by this extraordinary run rate. 'Not at all,' he answered, 'this is what happens at home every Saturday.'

Certainly, Lord's had never previously seen a Saturday like that of 7 September 1963 when Sussex and Worcestershire arrived with their supporters for the first Gillette Cup Final. Coach parties poured in

The first Cup Final at Lord's, 1963. Ted Dexter takes the Cup for Sussex.

Opposite: Lancashire's David Hughes batting in brighter weather.

from the country. Purveyors of football-style rosettes did a roaring trade at the gates, and as the afternoon wore on, the full-throated roars normally associated with the football stadium were heard resounding around the headquarters of cricket. Ted Dexter's Sussex men won the Cup; Worcestershire's Norman Gifford collected the first Cup Final Man-of-the-Match award, and one-day cricket was well and truly launched.

Or was it? An editorial in *The Cricketer*, while welcoming many features of the new-style game, hoped that the authorities would not be 'over impressed with the merits of one-day cricket'. It underlined the negative aspects inherent in the new version of cricket – defensive field-placings and 'the use of seam bowling to the almost total exclusion of spin'. It insisted that a balance needed to be struck between tradition and novelty. Besides, there lingered in the minds of many older cricket supporters the suspicion that the new one-day game was not really cricket, but rather an artificial variant designed to increase gate revenues.

LANCASHIRE LIGHTS THE TORCH
FOR LIMITED-OVER CRICKET

What the new one-day game needed in order to establish itself was a great cricket match. This was forthcoming at Old Trafford in the summer of 1971 when Lancashire met Gloucestershire in the Gillette Cup semi-finals. Curiously, this was one game where bad weather can be said to have made a positive contribution to the excitement. About an hour was lost to heavy rain in mid afternoon. Thus Lancashire, chasing a Gloucestershire total of 229, were destined to bat well into the evening. In reasonable daylight, David Lloyd and Barry Wood gave Lancashire a start of 61 runs for the first wicket. A tense dual between Clive Lloyd and Mike Procter followed, the former finally laying into the latter's fast, accurate bowling with 16 runs off 5 balls before he was bowled by Mortimore. Then a collapse started and the light began to fail.

When Lancashire's number nine, David Hughes, came to the wicket 25 runs were needed with four overs remaining – not an impossible asking rate in the right circumstances, but in the pavilion and in the buildings around the ground the lights had come on. The conditions were not dissimilar to those for floodlit cricket – without the floodlights!

The match had been a to-and-fro struggle all day. Now it gained a dramatic new dimension with the approach of darkness. The match was televised, though in the last overs the players were only dimly visible. Viewers, used to watching umpires leading players from the field in comparatively well-illuminated conditions, were amazed at the courageous play of the cricketers. Indeed, never before in the history of the game had so much compelling cricket been played in so little light. It is in this context that David Hughes' assault on the Gloucestershire off-spinner John Mortimore must be adjudged a truly epic effort. He hit Mortimore for four, six, two, two, four and six in one over, leaving captain Jackie Bond to nudge a single for victory.

Hughes, Lancashire's present captain, won the Man-of-the-Match award, though it is doubtful whether anyone had a clear view of the presentation. Yet in the darkness, Hughes had lit a torch for the cause of one-day cricket which may never be extinguished.

The Gillette Cup Final at Lord's a year later further endorsed one-day cricket as a potential source of great cricket, rather than mere speeded-up play. Clive Lloyd's dazzling 126, which won the Cup for Lancashire, was sufficient to convert this doubter. In how many conventional matches, it had to be asked, had one seen a bowler of Bob Willis' pace being driven casually back over his head for sixes?

AN ACCIDENTAL START

FOR ONE-DAY INTERNATIONALS

One-day international cricket owes its inception primarily to the weather. The Third Test at Melbourne scheduled for 30 December 1970 was a washout; but all was not lost. Sir Donald Bradman, almost as influential an administrator as he had been a batsman, acted decisively to restore the financial damage. With the consent of the English authorities he layed on an extra Test, bringing the number in the series to an unprecedented seven. More momentously, although Sir Don perhaps did not realize he was making history, he also authorized the first one-day international between two fully representative sides.

A heartening 46,000 spectators paid 33,323 Australian dollars to watch what Tony Greig has described as 'the match that changed modern cricket'. It was not a spectacular game. England scored 190 and Australia won the game with five wickets to spare, a result calculated to endear the new version of cricket to the Australian crowd. The match was also the first to see prize money, donated by Rothmans, changing hands. The winners collected $:A2400 and the losers $:A1200. As the Man of the Match with a top score of 82, John Edrich earned $:A200.

So it was that four unremitting days of rain, combined with the spectators' obvious appreciation of the experiment, launched what is now a regular series of fixtures on any international tour – in Australia, almost to the extinction of conventional Tests.

THE CHALLENGE OF THE FIRST WORLD CUP

Despite the encouraging omens, there were many who doubted that the first World Cup, due to be played in England in 1975, would prove a success. These sceptics had in mind a much earlier multinational event staged in 1912 – the ill-fated Triangular Tournament. The imaginative concept had been to bring the world's (then) three Test nations – England, Australia and South Africa – into contention over a single summer.

In the event, the weather was bad and South Africa were below par as competitors. Moreover, a players' strike had deprived Australia of

A closely contested game. Boyce kicks for 2 and Marsh is run out in the Prudential Cup Final, Australia *v* West Indies at Lord's, June 1975.

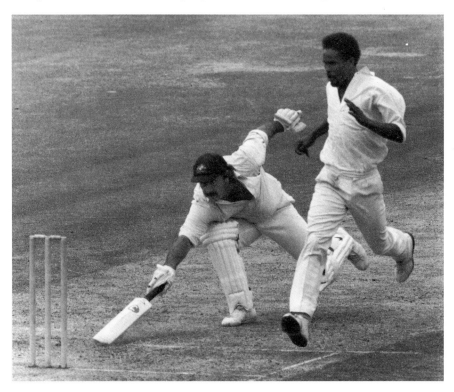

Julien successfully appeals against Rick McCosker in the same match. Centurion Clive Lloyd raises both hands in expectation.

many of its stars. But the essential reason for the experiment's failure was the fact that English crowds were not prepared to part with money to watch two teams of 'foreigners' like Australia and South Africa playing one another. The tournament yielded a net profit of £400.

The Prudential World Cup in England in 1975 clearly demonstrated that English spectators were now prepared to watch any number of overseas sides playing each other, so long as the cricket was entertaining. The qualifying rounds produced some enthralling cricket and one 'cliff-hanger' in the Pakistan v West Indies game at The Oval.

Pakistan scored 266 and West Indies were 203 for 9 when last man

Andy Roberts joined wicket-keeper Deryck Murray – 64 runs short of victory. At this point, Pakistan's captain, Majid Khan, made a tactical error only possible under the rules of limited-over cricket. Sarfraz Nawaz had ripped through the early West Indies batting. Now, with his allotted overs running out, Majid kept him on in the conviction that he would soon capture the last wicket. But Sarfraz ran out of steam, and overs. The Pakistan captain found himself in the embarrassing position of having to use a leg-spinner to bowl the last over. West Indies were off the hook and home with an incredible victory.

There were few, if any, empty seats when West Indies met Australia at Lord's in the final. The match was enriched by another glorious century by Clive Lloyd – 102 out of West Indies' total of 291. Australia made a great fight back. The fever pitch reached can be judged by the number of run-outs: five Australians were deemed to be short of the crease out of the eight wickets captured by West Indies. The victors were West Indies by 17 runs. Clive Lloyd was presented with the Cup and the Man-of-the-Match award by Prince Philip. All this and a jubilant pitch invasion effectively banished the spectre of the 1912 Triangular Tournament.

A SIGNIFICANT SHIFT

IN THE BALANCE OF WORLD POWER

Eight years later at another sell-out final at Lord's, India defied all probability by snatching the World Cup from under West Indies' nose. Before the match they had been 66 to 1 outsiders, according to the tote. For the sub-continent this was perhaps an even more important cricket match than The Oval victory over England in 1971. By gaining the title of world champions, India lifted the hearts of millions who did not differentiate too precisely between one-day internationals and conventional Tests.

The competitors in the 1983 World Cup, photographed at Lord's, June 1983.

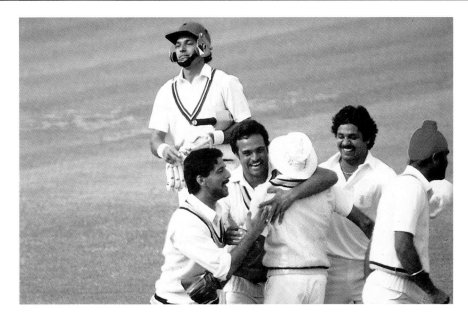

The balance of power is shifting. Bacchus is out. India's victory is nearer.

The wider cricketing world was delighted, too, because India's victory was a triumph of well-directed medium pace over numbing speed. It was, in a sense, a 'tortoise and hare' contest, with the West Indies racing arrogantly, if not foolhardily, towards India's unimpressive total of 183 and with India's seamers slowly picking up wickets with balls that did a little bit each way – until, suddenly, they were being carried shoulder high to the pavilion.

The Man of the Match was adjudged by Mike Brearley to be M. Amarnath, a man who had done a little with the bat and a little more with the ball, as the scorecard illustrates. What it cannot show is captain Kapil Dev racing backwards to the square-leg boundary to snatch down one Viv Richards swipe too many.

Sharma grabs a stump as the race for the pavilion begins.

Cheers for India!

PRUDENTIAL WORLD CUP FINAL, 1983

INDIA *v* WEST INDIES

Played at Lord's, 25 June
Result: India won by 43 runs

INDIA		WEST INDIES	
S.M. Gavaskar, c Dujon, b Roberts	2	C.G. Greenidge, b Sandhu	1
K. Srikkanth, lbw b Marshall ..	38	D.L. Haynes, c Binny, b Madan Lal....................	13
M. Amarnath, b Holding	26	I.V.A. Richards, c Kapil Dev, b Madan Lal	33
Yashpal Sharma, c sub, b Gomes	11	C.H. Lloyd, c Kapil Dev, b Binny	8
S.M. Patil, c Gomes, b Garner .	27	H.A. Gomes, c Gavaskar, b Madan Lal	5
Kapil Dev, c Holding, b Gomes.	15	S.F.A. Bacchus, c Kirmani, b Sandhu	8
K.B.J. Azad, c Garner, b Roberts	0	P.J. Dujon, b Amarnath	25
R.M.H. Binny, c Garner, b Roberts	2	M.D. Marshall, c Gavaskar, b Amarnath................	18
Madan Lal, b Marshall.......	17	A.M.E. Roberts, lbw b Kapil Dev	4
S.M.H. Kirmani, b Holding ...	14	J. Garner, not out...........	5
B.S. Sandhu, not out	11	M.A. Holding, lbw b Amarnath.	6
B 5, l-b 5, w 9, n-b 1	20	l-b 4, w 10.............	14
Total (54.4 overs)	183	Total (52 overs)......	140

Fall of wickets: 1–2, 2–59, 3–90, 4–92, 5–110, 6–111, 7–130, 8–153, 9–161, 10–183.

Fall of wickets: 1–5, 2–50, 3–57, 4–66, 5–66, 6–76, 7–119, 8–124, 9–126, 10–140.

BOWLING ANALYSIS

WEST INDIES	O	M	R	W	INDIA	O	M	R	W
Roberts	10	3	32	3	Kapil Dev........	11	4	21	1
Garner	12	4	24	1	Sandhu..........	9	1	32	2
Marshall.........	11	1	24	2	Madan Lal	12	2	31	3
Holding	9.4	2	26	2	Binny...........	10	1	23	1
Gomes	11	1	49	2	Amarnath........	7	0	12	3
Richards.........	1	0	8	0	Azad	3	0	7	0

Umpires: H.D. Bird and B.J. Meyer

Opposite: Kapil Dev, the unexpected Cup winner.

England takes the field at Calcutta.

THE CENTRE MOVES EASTWARDS

The result of the 1983 World Cup brought about a significant shift in the orientation of international cricket. As no one will need reminding, the 1987 Reliance World Cup was played in India and Pakistan, India's status as world champions being the clinching argument for the change of venue. Again, as readers will recall, an India *v* Pakistan final was anticipated. Yet some natural disappointment that the finalists turned out to be England and Australia did not mar the success of the competition. In this sense, the well-attended Anglo-Australian final at

Mike Gatting's fatal reverse sweep.

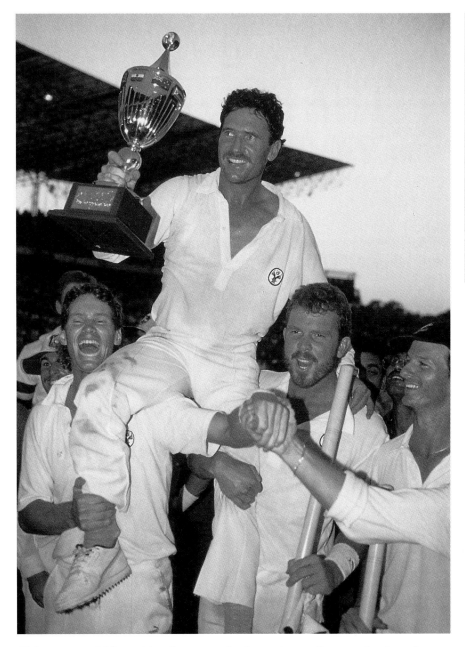

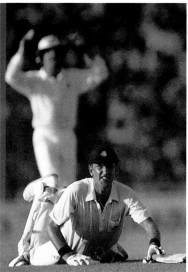

England slip up on the road to victory in the Calcutta Final. Bill Athey is the batsman.

Australia – another unexpected Cup winner in a great contest.

Calcutta could be said to have marked another milestone in the advance of one-day internationals, if not of international understanding itself. Indeed, it seems today almost as if one-day cricket has history on its side, while bad luck and bad tempers seem to dog conventional Tests. It is to be hoped that this is undue pessimism resulting from the England *v* Pakistan and New Zealand series.

It is doubtful whether one-day cricket will ever be able to match Tests such as those at The Oval in 1902 or Headingley and Edgbaston in 1981 for sustained interest and excitement. Yet it does have the inherent advantage of ensuring a result. Again, in its more limited time span the success or failure of individual performers seems to count for more. All might have been different for West Indies in Group B if Viv Richards had not slashed so contemptuously at a straight one from Eddie Hemmings. India could have been finalists if Kapil Dev had watched the ball a little more carefully as he swept the same bowler for a soaring catch to Mike Gatting at square-leg. Similarly, Gatting himself could have led England to the world title had he not indulged in that thoughtless reverse sweep against change-bowler Allan Border in the Calcutta final. The drama of one-day cricket has the potential to change the game even more radically than it has done to date.

5
THE ROOTS OF CONTROVERSY

Controversy is not exactly a recent phenomenon in international cricket, though to listen to some commentators one might be tempted to think otherwise. Unhappily, open dissension and even violence are traceable almost to the beginnings of meetings between nations. There has always lurked the danger that a game of cricket may be mistaken in some quarters for a battle of loyalties.

THE ASHES CONTEST POSTPONED
BY CROWD INTERFERENCE

It seemed a sensible idea to include an English umpire in the party when Lord Harris' England tourists sailed for Australia in the autumn of 1878. As we have already noticed, such exchanges of officials are now widely canvassed as a means of reducing controversy. But exactly the opposite effect was produced by George Coulthard's visit to Australia.

Trouble erupted in the second match against New South Wales at Sydney Cricket Ground when Coulthard, whose verdicts had already

Lord Harris' team before departure to Australia. Trouble awaited them at Sydney.

been the subject of some crowd unease, adjudged W.L. Murdoch run out in the state's second innings. Now the crowd became decidedly restive and, to add fuel to the sparks, the New South Wales captain, David Gregory, took the unprecedented step of walking onto the field with a demand that Coulthard be replaced for incompetence. Obliged to debate the matter in the glare of the arena, Lord Harris refused to oblige, whereupon Gregory far surpassed any of Mike Gatting's alleged offences at Faisalabad and called his batsmen from the field. This was the trigger for a pitch invasion of a ferocity never since paralleled in Anglo-Australian encounters.

Lord Harris, stump in hand, defended himself from the leaders of the mob. The police, backed by members of the England team, arrived in the nick of time to save him from serious injury. The assailants were led away on the arm of the law and Gregory, on mature reflection, allowed his batsmen to return to the crease.

This turbulent match had an immediate bearing on Anglo-Australian cricket relationships. It seems clear that when an Australian team under W.L. Murdoch visited England in 1880, Lord Harris used his influence to deny the visitors a Test match. Indeed, the tourists were so short of matches that they were compelled at one stage to advertise for fixtures. Only in September did Lord Harris relent. A team which included the Grace brothers and various amateurs, recalled from the grouse moors, was lucky to win the first Test match ever played in England by 5 wickets.

The punishment continued in 1882. Again the visiting Australians were permitted only a single Test. This time Australia won by 7 runs a match which would have received major coverage in this volume had the tale not so often been told. In any case, the result produced a profound shock in English cricketing circles. 'In affectionate memory of English cricket which died at The Oval on 29th August 1882,' announced the famous obituary in *The Sporting Times*. 'N.B. The body will be cremated and the ashes taken to Australia.' Now the running battle of the Ashes was well and truly joined.

A riot in Sydney had significantly delayed the most famous continuous contest in cricket. It also underlined the fact that international games can arouse the fiercest passions.

The First Test *v* Australia in England, The Oval, September 1880. Lord Harris used his influence to delay this historic encounter.

Douglas Jardine with India's captain, C.K. Naidu, at Bombay in 1933. The bumpers were to fly in this series too.

THE JARDINE FACTOR

Douglas Jardine was never enamoured of Australian crowds, and his reservations were heartily reciprocated, even before the Bodyline series. When the Surrey batsman was touring with A.P.F. Chapman's team in 1928/9 he was already attracting the odd catcall. As Jack Fingleton tells us, the average Australian spectator could never understand why a man privileged to wear his country's cap insisted on turning out for England in the striped colours of the Harlequin Club. They though it betrayed a kind of snobbish contempt for the Test arena. As for what Jardine thought, Sir Pelham Warner himself was to write to a friend: 'He is a queer fellow. When he sees a cricket ground with an Australian on it he goes mad.'

Perhaps one reason why Jardine's Bodyline tactics produced such a furious reaction from the Australian public was that they were accompanied by a personal demeanour that indicated the utmost distaste for Australian crowds and even Australian cricketers.

BUMPER DEVELOPMENTS

How far was Douglas Jardine responsible for introducing intimidation into Test cricket? We learn that the bumper was frowned upon in the game's golden age from the famous anecdote of 'the ball that was bowled through W.G.'s beard'. Historians are divided as to whether the ball actually passed through or merely brushed the most celebrated beard in cricket; but there is no doubt that the culprit was Ernest Jones, a young fast bowler with Harry Trott's 1896 Australian team in England. The significant point of the story is that Jones felt bound to apologize with the immortal words, 'Sorry, Doctor, she slipped.'

Sir Stanley Jackson suffered a cracked rib from a Jones lifter in the same match (Lord Sheffield's XI *v* the Australians) and was also to receive a handsome apology. 'Within a month of Sheffield Park,' he wrote, 'I faced Jones at Lord's in the MCC match, and he came up to me and said "I am terribly sorry", and he clasped my hand in a vice-like grip that left me wondering which was the more painful – my hand or broken ribs.' Jackson adds a revealing footnote to this incident. 'Trott took Jones in hand and made him into a very fine bowler. He made him shorten his run and taught him the value of length and control.' In other words, the short-pitched delivery was not, in this period, considered a respectable weapon.

We have noted G.L. Jessop's comment on the short-pitching tendency of Jack Gregory, the spearhead of Warwick Armstrong's 1921 Australians, and it could well be that following the catharsis of the First World War the bumpers began to fly more freely. However, the Australian attack was soon to be based predominantly on the spin of Grimmett and O'Reilly, while England was dependent on the medium pace of Maurice Tate with fast, but not yet furious, support from Harold Larwood. Not so much as a querulous murmur was raised at these combinations.

In this context, it can be seen that Jardine's tactics of persistent short-pitching on the line of the batsman, rather than the wicket, were calculated to create a sensation, even without the other essential feature of Bodyline – the packed leg-side field that made even self-defence risky.

ADELAIDE, 1933 – BODYLINE'S HIGH TIDE

Douglas Jardine's brand-new Bodyline weapon was unveiled at the First Sydney Test in 1932 where it was almost, but not quite, demolished by Stan McCabe with a courageous 187 not out. By the time the teams came to Adelaide for the Third Test with a victory apiece, the new method of attack was already notorious. That Jardine meant to

An express delivery from Harold Larwood.

intensify the Bodyline treatment was signalled before a ball was bowled, in the selection of the England team. The Nawab of Pataudi, who had scored a century at Sydney, was replaced by Eddie Paynter. Pataudi had declined to join the ring of men crowding the batsman on the leg side in the previous Melbourne Test. 'I see that His Highness is a conscientious objector,' Jardine had observed icily before ordering Hedley Verity to fill the gap.

If Bodyline had created a stir before Adelaide, it now provoked a major imperial crisis. In Australia's first innings, Woodfull, the captain, was struck a sickening blow above the heart from a short-pitched ball from Larwood. It was at this point that Jardine fully earned his reputation as a man of cold steel. In defiance of a roaring crowd, he immediately switched his field to the packed leg side which had now become synonymous with intimidation. Nothing could have better illustrated the ruthless purpose of Bodyline.

Later, back in the pavilion, the England managers Pelham Warner and Mr R.C.N. Palairet called at the Australian dressing room to express their sympathy with the injured Woodfull, now stretched out under towels. They were told curtly, 'There are two teams out there, and only one of them is playing cricket!' Warner and Palairet withdrew without further comment. But the incident was leaked to the press, by either Bradman or twelfth man L.P. O'Brien, and the following morning every Australian knew how matters stood. Next morning, too, the Aussie wicket-keeper, Oldfield, deflected a bumper from Larwood on to his head. Even though Oldfield gallantly signalled that he was at fault, the atmosphere at the Adelaide Oval was now charged to explosive levels.

The one man who could have defused the situation was Pelham Warner, the most respected authority in cricket. He chose to do nothing, at least until he got back to England, leaving the Australian Board of Control to fire off an angry cable to the MCC to which an equally uncompromising message was returned: 'We, Marylebone Cricket Club, deplore your cable etc., etc.'

Oldfield deflects a ball from Larwood onto his head.

ENGLAND v AUSTRALIA, 1933

Third Test match played at Adelaide, 13, 14, 16, 17, 18 and 19 January
Result: England won by 338 runs

ENGLAND

H. Sutcliffe, c Wall, b O'Reilly .	9	c sub (O'Brien), b Wall	7
D.R. Jardine (capt), b Wall	3	lbw b Ironmonger	56
W.R. Hammond, c Oldfield, b Wall	2	b Bradman	85
L.E.G. Ames, b Ironmonger . . .	3	b O'Reilley	69
M. Leyland, b O'Reilly	83	c Wall, b Ironmonger	42
R.E.S. Wyatt, c Richardson, b Grimmett	78	c Wall, b O'Reilly	49
E. Paynter, c Fingleton, b Wall .	77	not out	1
G.O. Allen, lbw b Grimmett . . .	15	lbw b Grimmett	15
H. Verity, c Richardson, b Wall.	45	lbw b O'Reilly	40
W. Voce, b Wall.	8	b O'Reilly	8
H. Larwood, not out.	3	c Bradman, b Ironmonger	8
B 1, l-b 7, n-b 7.	15	B 17, l-b 11, n-b 4	32
Total	341	Total	412

Fall of wickets. First innings: 1–4, 2–16, 3–16, 4–30, 5–186, 6–196, 7–228, 8–324, 9–336, 10–341. Second innings: 1–7, 2–91, 3–123, 4–154, 5–245, 6–296, 7–394, 8–395, 9–403, 10–412.

AUSTRALIA

J.H. Fingleton, c Ames, b Allen.	0	b Larwood	0
W.M. Woodfull (capt), b Allen .	22	not out	73
D.G. Bradman, c Allen, b Larwood	8	c and b Verity	66
S.J. McCabe, c Jardine, b Larwood	8	c Leyland, b Allen	7
W.H. Ponsford, b Voce.	85	c Jardine, b Larwood	3
V.Y. Richardson, b Allen	28	c Allen, b Larwood	21
W.A. Oldfield, retired, hurt. . . .	41	absent, hurt	0
C.V. Grimmett, c Voce, b Allen.	10	b Allen	6
T.W. Wall, b Hammond	6	b Allen	0
W.J. O'Reilley, b Larwood	0	b Larwood	5
H. Ironmonger, not out.	0	b Allen	0
B 2, l-b 11, n-b 1	14	B 4, l-b 2, w 1, n-b 5	12
Total	222	Total	193

Fall of wickets. First innings: 1–1, 2–18, 3–34, 4–51, 5–131, 6–194, 7–212, 8–222, 9–222. Second innings: 1–3, 2–12, 3–100, 4–116, 5–171, 6–183, 7–183, 8–192, 9–193.

BOWLING ANALYSIS

AUSTRALIA

	O	M	R	W		O	M	R	W
Wall.	34.1	10	72	5	Wall.	29	6	75	1
O'Reilly	50	19	82	2	O'Reilly	50.3	21	79	4
Ironmonger.	20	6	50	1	Ironmonger.	57	21	87	3
Grimmett	28	6	94	2	Grimmett	35	9	74	1
McCabe	14	3	28	0	McCabe	16	0	42	0
					Bradman	4	0	23	1

O'Reilly, 4 n-b   Wall, 2 n-b
Wall, 3 n-b   O'Reilly, 1 n-b
                      McCabe, 1 n-b

ENGLAND

	O	M	R	W		O	M	R	W
Larwood.	25	6	55	3	Larwood.	19	3	71	4
Allen	23	4	71	4	Allen	17.2	5	50	4
Hammond	17.4	4	30	1	Hammond	9	3	27	0
Voce	14	5	21	1	Voce	4	1	7	0
Verity.	16	7	31	0	Verity.	20	12	26	1

Voce, 1 n-b   Allen, 1 w, 2 n-b
                   Verity, 1 n-b
                   Larwood, 2 n-b

A heroes' welcome for Voce, Larwood and Jardine in Nottingham. Disciplining would come later.

The crisis now assumed political proportions. Questions were raised in the Canberra Parliament. It was asked, with some justice, why a dominion which had sent the cream of her manhood to fight and die for England in her war with the Kaiser's Germany deserved to see her Test players systematically battered by a vengeful Scotsman. There was even talk of severing the Empire connection and declaring a republic. This was how far things had been taken by a method of bowling designed to curb the run-scoring of Bradman.

Eventually, the MCC was bound to take note. Jardine, who had been enthusiastically welcomed home with the Ashes and a 4–1 series victory, was encouraged to resign the England captaincy. Intimidatory bowling, in any shape or form, was outlawed by the time the Australians arrived in 1934. Tragically for English cricket, Harold Larwood was driven from the Test scene for refusing to confess that he had only been obeying orders. By recanting, his partner Bill Voce was finally readmitted to the England Test side in 1936.

Yet as far as the future of Test cricket was concerned, the damage had already been done. It is true that the packed leg-side field, waiting to snatch the ball from the parrying bat, would henceforth be banned from cricket. Nevertheless, the progress of short-pitched bowling was to trace a rising graph.

THE RIPPLES SPREAD

Australia waited only until they had the necessary fast bowlers (Lindwall and Miller) to make things uncomfortable for England batsmen. One illustration of this is an item in the scorecard for the First Test at Nottingham in 1948, which reads: 'Compton hit wicket b. Miller 184'. The truth was that this potentially match-saving innings was brought to an end by Compton being obliged to fall on his stumps.

Keith Miller had bowled him a rearing bumper which offered few other options. This was a Test match when it became the English crowd's turn to roar its disapproval of the head-high ball. Yet no England batsman was in a position to demand, as W.G. Grace had done after the 'beard' incident, 'Here, what is all this?'. Douglas Jardine had forfeited their right of protest.

Keith Miller takes his punishment like a man in a 1956 match in England. Against West Indies in 1950 he would hand it out.

THE PULVERIZATION OF WEST INDIES

The 1951/2 Test series with West Indies in Australia saw an ironic twist in the tale of intimidation and controversy. The series took place shortly after the West Indian triumph in England in 1950, and was billed as a battle for the world championship. It seems to have been Australia's aim to put in a pre-emptive strike against a dangerous new rival before it gained overwhelming strength. In any case, the Tests witnessed Keith Miller 'take out' Sonny Ramadhin with a flailing bat, and the pulverization of the West Indies' batting line-up by the daunting pace of Ray Lindwall and Keith Miller. Under anti-intimidatory legislation, the umpires would surely have been justified in calling a halt when, at the Fifth Test in Sydney, with the series already won, Lindwall increased his bumper rate to a controversial two an over against an injured batsman, Everton Weekes.

Now, influential Australian opinion was obliged to scold its own bowlers. 'I saw Lindwall that same afternoon,' Bill O'Reilly informed his friend, Jack Fingleton. 'I told him I thought that his tactics were bloody shocking, that he had made himself look cheap, and that I had written so for the next morning's *Herald*.'

'Give us Miller and let us play Australia again!' demanded the West Indian captain, John Goddard, after his 4–1 series defeat. He might have said Wes Hall, Charlie Griffith, Andy Roberts, Michael Holding,

Brian Close and John Edrich face the bombardment at Old Trafford, 1976.

Joel Garner or Malcolm Marshall, because these were the fast men who would eventually shift the balance of power. Indeed, one wonders if it is too fanciful to suggest that it was this bruising experience against Australia which began the West Indian search for aggressive pace at the expense of spin.

WEST INDIES WARNED

The scene changes to Old Trafford in 1976. England, needing a matter of 552 to win, opened their second innings with John Edrich and the forty-five-year-old Brian Close. Possibly it was the strokelessness of the pair that provoked an extra touch of venom from the West Indian fast bowlers (it took Close 77 minutes to move from 1 to 2). Whatever the cause, both men were submitted to one of the most savage assaults upon batsmen ever witnessed in England. Eventually umpire Bill Alley raised a warning finger at Michael Holding, as he had much earlier been entitled to do under the law. It was certainly too late to save Close from serious bruising, though he may have been lucky to escape concussion.

The following morning's papers were strong in their condemnation of the West Indian tactics and of the seeming complacency of umpires Alley and Budd. Test cricket took another crucial step towards the age of crash helmets.

But perhaps the root of the trouble had been planted at Adelaide, in January 1933. History suggests that before Jardine and Bodyline, extreme fast bowling had been merely one way of getting wickets. Ever afterwards, it would tend to be associated with controversy.

6
FATE TAKES A HAND

Cricket is a glorious game with one serious defect – it is vulnerable to the weather, most especially to rain. Sometimes (but not too often), the intervention of the elements has been beneficial. For instance, the rain that washed out the Second Test at Melbourne in 1970 was instrumental in bringing about the popular concept of one-day international cricket. Similarly, somewhere in the season of 1871 was a ruined fixture that decided the authorities to introduce the first form of pitcn-covering in the following year.

THE GREAT CRICKETING DAY THAT NEVER WAS

The downpour that eradicated the final day of the Bicentenary match at Lord's in 1987 can be said to have done cricket a grave disservice. Up to that point, spectators and viewers had had a glimpse of top-class cricket as it was meant to be played – the best players in all departments in friendly but avid rivalry. By the fourth day we had forgotten we were indifferent to who won (the choice was MCC or the Rest of the World) and had become totally absorbed in the cricket. For our special delectation were splendid centuries by the four 'Gs' – Gooch, Gatting, Gavaskar and Greenidge – the superb fielding of Roger Harper and the

'Cricket is vulnerable to the weather.' A hailstorm at Arundel World Cup friendly, Australia *v* New Zealand, June 1983.

The great day for cricket that never was! The scene at Lord's on the last day of the Bicentenary Test.

spectacle of great bowlers such as Richard Hadlee, Malcolm Marshall, Kapil Dev and Imran Khan waiting their turn, like jets at Heathrow, for use of the runway.

Although we didn't really mind who won, the match on Monday evening was fascinatingly poised. The Rest of the World needed over 300 to win; but no one could doubt that they would make a tremendous fight of it, notwithstanding the fact that Malcolm Marshall of MCC had flattened Sunil Gavaskar's off stump for 0 in the evening gloom. Then it rained buckets, and all we could do was imagine how the final day might have been. It is tempting to believe that this last day might have reminded the cricket world that one day is not necessarily sufficient for thrilling cricket. It might also have reminded the players (for there were some very influential characters in the two sides) just how a five-day contest ought to be conducted. The weather can change the course of cricket as decisively as the men.

Worcester cricket ground
under water, April 1987.

THE CENTENARY TEST FORCES A RE-THINK

The Centenary Test at Lord's in September 1980 should, logically, have been played at The Oval, for the game marked the first Test match (against Australia) ever to be played in England on that ground, in 1880. Perhaps if the match had been played at the original venue it might not have suffered so adversely from the weather, for reasons we shall shortly suggest. As it was, the fixture saw all kinds of unpalatable goods placed in an important cricket 'shop window'.

Once again, rain was a major culprit; it rained heavily on the Friday night. However, a dedicated ground staff worked through the small hours to preserve the wicket for Saturday's play. At the time scheduled for the start, the sun was shining. The rain had stopped seven hours before. Yet there was no play before lunch and only promises of further pitch inspections after lunch. Outside the ground, a sizeable crowd of non-ticket-holders waited for admission. The wicket itself had been covered and was ready for play but, apparently, two worn patches down the Lord's slope on the Tavern boundary provided treacherous footholds for fielders. In the waiting crowd were old Test cricketers and enthusiasts who had crossed the world to be present at this great occasion.

Sooner or later, the crowd was bound to tire of watching the sunlight playing on the vacant Lord's grass. Its temper was not improved by persistent loudspeaker announcements from a hired actor with Richard Burton overtones who, though formally apologetic at the start, increasingly began to scold the crowd for its impatience.

Now significant divisions began to appear in the match management. Head groundsman Jim Fairbrother's men, who had toiled through the darkness to save the day, began to confide to anyone within earshot that the field was perfectly fit for play. Unkind words, some of them unprintable, were expressed concerning the alleged obstinacy of umpires Dicky Bird and David Constant, although it was later claimed that it was the England captain Ian Botham who was unwilling to risk his fielders on the sticky patches.

When the inevitable explosion came, it was in the least expected of quarters. Returning from, or setting out for, yet another pitch inspection, Botham and Greg Chappell were jostled and the umpires set upon by MCC members in flamboyantly identifiable club ties. Umpire Bird was nearly felled by the fury of these privileged cricket lovers, and Constant was taken by the throat.

These unimaginable happenings were followed by a surprising lack of imagination on the part of the organizing authorities. The reluctant and bedraggled umpires were finally ordered to commence play at 3.45.

The groundstaff toil to save a major fixture.

The players appeared to hollow cheering, only to disappear half an hour later for the statutory tea interval. The players had had four and three-quarter hours to gorge themselves with tea and cake!

The match was extended by an hour on the remaining days, yet the Cornhill Centenary Test Match ended tranquilly with a Boycott century and a draw. The match was far from being the success anticipated and compared unfavourably with the splendid Melbourne Centenary game in 1977. The elements and the miscalculations and misbehaviour of men had combined to destroy, perhaps forever, the image of the MCC member as a paragon of dignity and restraint.

Yet there were compensatory benefits. It would seem that it was this unhappy game that finally persuaded the authorities that cricket should be organized for the benefit of the spectators rather than for the convenience of officials and players. New methods of pitch-drying were investigated, and at Lord's an investment in additional covering may, with luck, have ensured that 'worn patches' are never again responsible for robbing a sunny day of cricket.

Anyone for cricket? Groundsman Jim Fairbrother talks prospects with the umpires, and captains Botham and Greg Chappell.

RAIN, THE DAMPENER OF THE WILL TO WIN?

Weather shapes the attitudes of the various Test-playing nations. In England an unpredictable climate would appear to have made both officials and players more ready to accept a drawn game than is the case in, say, Australia. Whole Test matches have been washed out in England, including a vital one at Old Trafford in 1938, without any attempt being made, as Bradman successfully did in 1970/1, to rearrange the fixture. England never did understand what Warwick Armstrong was on about with his open newspaper and his 'fight to the finish' crusade back in 1921. Certainly, this acceptance of the vagaries of fate and the elements seems to have seeped through into the minds of England's present Test cricketers. The fact that at the start of the 1988 season they had failed to win one Test out of a possible thirteen may suggest that results themselves are insufficiently reverenced.

ENGLAND SWEPT TO AN OVAL VICTORY

Perhaps the greatest counter-attack ever mounted against the ravages of the weather took place on the final day of the Fifth Test match against Australia at The Oval in 1968. Rain had afflicted this Ashes series all

'New methods of pitch drying were investigated.' Left, heaters and, inset, helicopters at Worcester.

summer, to the extent that England, who looked to be the stronger team, came to The Oval one down with only the hope of a squared rubber to play for.

In perfect weather England scored 494, thanks largely to John Edrich's 164 and a momentous 158 from Basil D'Oliveira. Australia fought back to 324, their hopes sustained by a score of 133 from captain Bill Lawry in an Atlas-like role. England scurried to 181 all out, leaving Australia needing 352 to win in six hours thirty-five minutes. They were 86 for 5 at lunch-time on Tuesday when a massive thunderstorm broke over the ground, and England's captain Colin Cowdrey found himself staring at his reflection in an Oval lakeland.

It may be unfair to suggest that it was England's promising position that inspired the efforts that followed, though it must be questioned whether such zeal would have been apparent had Australia been in the driving seat. The head groundsman called for volunteers from the crowd, and brooms were issued to dozens of willing hands. As in one of those warm-hearted old Ealing comedies in which an entire community turns out to get a vintage steam engine back on the rails, The Oval ground was rapidly swept clear of water. Almost miraculously, play was restarted at a quarter to five.

Colin Cowdrey posted ten men around the sawdust-strewn wicket.

ENGLAND v AUSTRALIA, 1968

Fifth Test match played at The Oval, 22, 23, 24, 26, 27 August
Result: England won by 226 runs

ENGLAND

J.H. Edrich, b Chappell	164	c Lawry, b Mallett ... 17
C. Milburn, b Connolly	8	c Lawry, b Connolly ... 18
E.R. Dexter, b Gleeson	21	b Connolly ... 28
M.C. Cowdrey, lbw b Mallett	16	b Mallett ... 35
T.W. Graveney, c Redpath, b McKenzie	63	run out ... 12
B.L. D'Oliveira, c Inverarity, b Mallett	158	c Gleeson, b Connolly ... 9
A.P.E. Knott, c Jarman, b Mallett	28	run out ... 34
R. Illingworth, lbw b Connolly	8	b Gleeson ... 10
J.A. Snow, run out	4	c Sheahan, b Gleeson ... 13
D.L. Underwood, not out	9	not out ... 1
D.J. Brown, c Sheaham, b Gleeson	2	b Connolly ... 1
B 1, l-b 11, w 1	13	l-b 3 ... 3
Total	494	Total ... 181

Fall of wickets. First innings: 1–28, 2–84, 3–113, 4–238, 5–359, 6–421, 7–458, 8–468, 9–489, 10–494. Second innings: 1–23, 2–53, 3–67, 4–90, 5–114, 6–126, 7–149, 8–179, 9–179, 10–181.

AUSTRALIA

W.M. Lawry, c Knott, b Snow	133	c Milburn, b Brown ... 4
R.J. Inverarity, c Milburn, b Snow	1	lbw b Underwood ... 56
I.R. Redpath, c Cowdrey, b Snow	67	lbw b Underwood ... 8
I.M. Chappell, c Knott, b Brown	10	lbw b Underwood ... 2
K.D. Walters, c Knott, b Brown	5	c Knott, b Underwood ... 1
A.P. Sheahan, b Illingworth	14	c Snow, b Illingworth ... 24
B.N. Jarman, st Knott, b Illingworth	0	b D'Oliveira ... 21
G.D. McKenzie, b Brown	12	c Brown, b Underwood ... 0
A.A. Mallett, not out	43	c Brown, b Underwood ... 0
J.W. Gleeson, c Dexter, b Underwood	19	b Underwood ... 5
A.N. Connolly, b Underwood	3	not out ... 0
B 4, l-b 7, n-b 4	15	l-b 4 ... 4
Total	324	Total ... 125

Fall of wickets. First innings: 1–7, 2–136, 3–151, 4–161, 5–185, 6–188, 7–237, 8–269, 9–302, 10–324. Second innings: 1–4, 2–13, 3–19, 4–29, 5–65, 6–110, 7–110, 8–110, 9–120, 10–125.

BOWLING ANALYSIS

AUSTRALIA

	O	M	R	W		O	M	R	W
McKenzie	40	8	87	1	McKenzie	4	0	14	0
Connolly	57	12	127	2	Connolly	22.4	2	65	4
Walters	6	2	17	0					
Gleeson	41.2	8	109	2	Gleeson	7	2	22	2
Mallett	36	11	87	3	Mallett	25	4	77	2
Chappell	21	5	54	1					

ENGLAND

	O	M	R	W		O	M	R	W
Snow	35	12	67	3	Snow	11	5	22	0
Brown	22	5	63	3	Brown	8	3	19	1
Illingworth	48	15	87	2	Illingworth	28	18	29	1
Underwood	54.3	21	89	2	Underwood	31.3	19	50	7
D'Oliveira	4	2	3	0	D'Oliveira	5	4	1	1

Umpires: C.S. Elliott and A.E. Fagg

D'Oliveira made the breakthrough by sneaking one under Jarman's bat and Derek Underwood did the rest, finally bowling Inverarity with five minutes left for play.

Spectators help mop up the waterlogged pitch at The Oval during the 5th and final Test, England v Australia, 1968.

The Australians could have raised a few eyebrows. However, they sportingly conceded that, considering how often weather had foiled England during the series, justice had been done. That rain had not been permitted to claim another draw was fortunate for English cricket, which had almost begun to despair of doing justice to itself in Tests with Australia.

Unhappily, events immediately following the match had other more significant ramifications. The following day, the England party to tour South Africa that winter was announced. Basil D'Oliveira, who had scored 185 at The Oval and had made the crucial breakthrough on Tuesday evening, was omitted, and in view of his Oval performance it was widely supposed that this was for political rather than cricketing reasons. As a result the long, acrimonious saga of the ending of Tests with South Africa began. Rain and zealous mopping-up apart, this was indeed a match that witnessed the start of a great change in the international cricketing scene.

THE MELBOURNE MYSTERY

The Third Test at Melbourne, 1954/5, will live forever in literature, and not simply because it witnessed a great victory for England and Frank Tyson. In Harold Pinter's play *The Birthday Party*, the protagonist is accused by two menacing strangers of, among other unlikely crimes, 'watering the wicket at Melbourne'.

The reference is to a mystifying happening during this mid 1950s

Test. On the Saturday of the match, ominous cracks began to appear on the Melbourne pitch which, in the experts' view, indicated the imminent disintegration of the wicket. A rough passage was forecast for England, who would be batting on the Monday, with an even less comfortable outlook for Australia, should they have to face Tyson and Statham on the track afterwards.

On Monday morning, however, the wicket had, amazingly, healed. The obvious inference was that the pitch had been watered and rolled over the weekend in contravention of the laws of Test cricket. This was vigorously denied by the Victorian Cricket Association. It was suggested that the intense heat had drawn up moisture from the underlying Yarra river; the possibility of natural 'sweating' was advanced as an alternative explanation. The mystery lingers, like that of the *Mary Celeste*. But there are still convinced advocates of the simple solution.

For Harold Pinter's many American students, that line in *The Birthday Party* must pose an even greater mystery. It is a pleasant fancy to think that in their investigations of the crime of 'watering the wicket at Melbourne', thousands of US professors and eager thesis writers may be led to an understanding of cricket, and even to pleasure in the game. In that case, Melbourne '54/5 will indeed have proved an influential Test match.

GEORGE DAVIS AND OTHER INCURSIONS

Protest, political or otherwise, has been as effective as the British weather in disrupting crucial Tests in the Indian sub-continent and the West Indies, but only once has its full effect been felt in England.

On the night of 18 August 1975, supporters of the 'George Davis is innocent' campaign made sufficient dents in the Headingley Test pitch to render it unfit for play. The match at this point was tantalizingly poised. Australia, with seven second innings remaining, needed to make 225 for victory. Rick McCosker was undefeated on 95, but both Chappell brothers were back in the pavilion. For Tony Greig's England team, the chances of squaring the rubber and ending a sequence of humiliating defeats at the hands of the old enemy looked at least as good as they had to Colin Cowdrey and his men before the rains had come at The Oval in 1968.

What were the administrators to do? With Australia one up in the four-match series, to declare an extra day or prepare a new wicket could seem to be favouring England, particularly the latter alternative, which could have given the England bowlers encouragement which had been lacking in the original track.

For the first time in the history of televised cricket, the nation's screens carried the message 'MATCH ABANDONED DUE TO VANDALISM ON PITCH'. As it turned out, rain intervened to dampen the impact of the George Davis brigade's protest. The last day of this Headingley Test would have been washed out even if the wicket had not been ruined by human agencies. By the same token, a dampener was placed on the uncomfortable issues raised by the episode.

For the record, Hitler's forces narrowly missed creating far greater devastation on a cricket pitch than that wrought by the George Davis fanatics. On 29 July 1944, a flying bomb nosed towards Lord's where the Army were playing the RAF. The players, umpires and spectators flattened themselves as the missile limped over the ground and exploded in nearby Albert Road. On the resumption of play, Lieutenant J.D. Robertson (later of England) hooked the first ball he received for a rousing six – a stroke which splendidly symbolized cricket's triumphant survival of five grim years of war. The alternative scenario could have been the extinction of a nucleus of players vital to the re-establishment of cricket when peace came. Yet the war was to rob the

Tony Greig and Ian Chappell
inspect the damage wrought by
the 'George Davis is innocent'
agitators.

national team of two bowlers who might have spared England galling defeats against Australia in the post-war period – Kenneth Farnes, killed in a flying accident, and Hedley Verity who fell in action in Sicily.

A 'SCOOP' FOR CRICKET LITERATURE

Let us end on a happy note, with a great match and a fortunate accident which was to benefit cricket in an unexpected way. In 1921 Neville Cardus was already a respected cricket writer with *The Manchester Guardian*, though not yet a household name. In August of that season he received a postcard from A.C. MacLaren, then long into his retirement. It contained the memorable words, 'I think I know how to beat Armstrong's lot; come and write about it for *The Guardian*.'

The match Cardus was urged to attend was A.C. MacLaren's XI *v* the Australians at Eastbourne. *The Guardian*'s sports editor was not enthusiastic about giving this fixture major coverage. Like everyone else in England that summer, he had formed the opinion that Armstrong's Australians could not be beaten, least of all by a scratch team led by a fifty-two-year-old veteran of the Victorian era. He exhorted his star reporter to cover Surrey *v* Yorkshire at The Oval, but somehow Cardus managed to persuade his editor that MacLaren should be heeded – not an easy job in view of the great man's disappointing track record in Test captaincy.

A.C. MacLaren and friends. The 'scratch' team that beat Australia and made the name of Neville Cardus.

Among the vacant seats at the Saffrons Ground at Eastbourne, Cardus watched MacLaren's team being bundled out for 43 after which the Australians, in a free-scoring mood, put 174 on the board by close of play. He wondered what on earth his editor would say. Indeed, we get the impression that reluctance to face this executive was one reason why Cardus lingered at Eastbourne. However, when he returned to the ground on Monday morning his bags were packed. Cardus advances another reason for his strange delay: he wanted to see his ageing hero face up to an Australian attack for the last time. But even as he watched, MacLaren's stumps were immediately uprooted by E.A. McDonald!

Neville Cardus was half-way to the exit when the sound of bat impacting confidently with ball drew him back. The veteran South African batsman Aubrey Faulkner, and the young Cambridge player Hubert Ashton, had embarked on a mighty stand that was to give MacLaren a second-innings total of 326 (Faulkner 153, Ashton 75). Cardus stayed at Eastbourne a further day and saw the Australians skittled out for 167, to give MacLaren an extraordinary victory by 28 runs. 'By my faith in MacLaren,' Neville Cardus wrote, 'I achieved this, the only "scoop" of my career.'

By the end of his career, the oft-defeated MacLaren had made his name as a giant-killer. Perhaps even more significantly for cricket, the match was the making of Neville Cardus, a man who, in his way, was to do as much to propagate the joy of cricket as any of the great players about whom he wrote so evocatively.

Incidentally, MacLaren's victory at Eastbourne provided Donald Bradman with one more record to aim at. Warwick Armstrong had failed by one game to establish an unbeaten record in England in 1921. In 1948, Bradman would take pains to ensure that a triumphant Australian progress was not ambushed again.

INDEX

189

PHOTOGRAPHIC ACKNOWLEDGEMENTS

The author and publishers would like to thank Adrian Murrell of Allsport Photographic Ltd for his help and advice in providing the colour pictures in this book and for suggesting alternative sources for the black and white photographs. The author and publishers would also like to thank the following sources for their help in providing black and white pictures:

Patrick Eager
Mary Evans Picture Library
Illustrated London News Picture Library
The Keystone Collection
Stephen Green, Curator of the Museum, Lords Cricket Ground
Graham Morris
National Portrait Gallery
Sport and General Press Agency
Olive Synge

Where there is more than one picture on a page, the credits start with the pictures furthest to the left and nearest the top of the page and work down each side.

Allsport Photographic Ltd
Pages 8, 9 (John Gichigi), 13, 18b (Simon Bruty), 19, 20a (Chris Cole), 21, 24, 36, 37a (John Gichigi), 37b, 40a, 46, 47b (Chris Cole), 49b (Chris Cole), 52a, 52b, 56, 58, 60, 65, 69, 71, 73, 75, 84, 90b, 95, 101a, 101b, 111, 112, 114b, 153, 156, 159, 166b (Chris Cole), 167a (Chris Cole), 179 inset (Russell Cheyne), 181.

Allsport/Adrian Murrell
Pages 20b, 32, 33, 35, 45, 47a, 48, 49a, 50, 51, 57, 64, 67, 68, 77, 79, 80, 81, 83, 85, 86, 87, 88a, 88b, 89, 90a, 91, 96, 97, 98a, 98b, 103, 104b, 105a, 105b, 106, 107 inset, 108a, 108b, 110, 130, 131, 132/133, 134/135, 137, 138, 162, 163a, 163b, 164, 165, 166a, 167b, 176, 177, 178/179, 180, 182/183, 183b.

The Museum, Lords Cricket Ground
Pages 11, 12, 15, 16, 18a, 25, 29, 38, 39, 59, 61, 63a, 63b, 72, 74, 76, 99, 100, 102, 104a, 119, 125, 128, 145, 147, 148, 148/149, 157, 168, 171, 172, 188.

The Keystone Collection
Pages 26, 41, 43, 44, 53, 55, 70, 92, 114a, 115, 116a, 116/117, 123, 124, 160, 161, 170, 174, 175, 185.

Sport and General Press Agency
Pages 30, 42a, 42b, 54, 120/121, 122, 152.

Illustrated London News Picture Library
Pages 127, 141, 143, 144.

Mary Evans Picture Library
Pages 17, 113, 169.

National Portrait Gallery
Page 23.

Patrick Eagar
Page 187.

Graham Morris
Page 93.

Olive Synge
Page 10.